Frederic William Farrar

The witness of history to Christ

five sermons preached before the University of Cambridge

Frederic William Farrar

The witness of history to Christ

five sermons preached before the University of Cambridge

ISBN/EAN: 9783744745482

Printed in Europe, USA, Canada, Australia, Japan

Cover: Foto ©Lupo / pixelio.de

More available books at **www.hansebooks.com**

THE

WITNESS OF HISTORY TO CHRIST

FIVE SERMONS PREACHED BEFORE THE UNIVERSITY OF CAMBRIDGE

BEING THE HULSEAN LECTURES FOR THE YEAR 1870

BY THE

REV. F. W. FARRAR, D.D., F.R.S.

CANON OF WESTMINSTER

London

MACMILLAN AND CO.

AND NEW YORK

1889

All Rights Reserved

TO THE

REV. W. THOMPSON, D.D.,
MASTER OF TRINITY COLLEGE, CAMBRIDGE,

THESE LECTURES

ARE GRATEFULLY AND RESPECTFULLY

DEDICATED.

PREFACE.

A SERIES of accidental circumstances has caused the publication of these Lectures to be long delayed, and renders it necessary to send them forth, even now, in a condition much less complete than I had originally intended and hoped. Among other things I have greatly wished to add, by way of Preface or Introduction, some further considerations upon the subjects with which the Lectures severally deal; but I am obliged to forego this intention. The Lectures were written while I was in a position which left me but little leisure for thought or study; but they are published amid the pressure of still more incessant occupations. I can only pray that with all their imperfections they may be accepted as a sincere and honest effort to strengthen in the minds of those who read them a faith in the great truths of Christianity; and their purpose will not have wholly failed if they impart to but one single soul a deeper conviction of the certainty of those doctrines which were once found competent to regenerate a diseased and perishing society, and which have lost no single element of their power to quicken, in the hearts of all those who faithfully accept them, the desire to spend a noble life, and the ability to bring that desire to good effect.

I have only to add that a great portion of the proof-sheets was corrected while I had no means of obtaining access to books, and another portion while I was suffering from the effects of a serious accident. I have done my best to ensure accuracy, but it is only too probable that a few *errata*—I hope not many—may have crept into the following pages from these causes.

F. W. F.

Marlborough College,
April 20, 1871.

CONTENTS.

I.
THE ANTECEDENT CREDIBILITY OF THE MIRACULOUS . 1

II.
THE ADEQUACY OF THE GOSPEL RECORDS . . . 47

III.
THE VICTORIES OF CHRISTIANITY 89

IV.
CHRISTIANITY AND THE INDIVIDUAL . . 127

V.
CHRISTIANITY AND THE RACE 165

APPENDICES.
APPENDIX A. *On the Diversity of Christian Evidences* 199
APPENDIX B. *Confucius* . . . 201
APPENDIX C. *Buddha* . . 203
APPENDIX D. *Comte* . 205

I.

THE ANTECEDENT CREDIBILITY OF THE MIRACULOUS.

Τὰ ἀδύνατα παρὰ ἀνθρώποις δυνατά ἐστι παρὰ τῷ Θεῷ.
Luke xviii. 27.

Τί ἄπιστον κρίνεται παρ' ὑμῖν, εἰ ὁ Θεὸς τοὺς νεκροὺς ἐγείρει;
Acts xxvi. 8.

Heb. II. 4.

God also bearing them witness, both with signs and wonders and with divers miracles, and gifts of the Holy Ghost, according to His own will.

HE, my brethren, who having been ordained to the ministry of the word, stands up to preach the gospel which his Master taught, ought to do so on all occasions with as little fear or misgiving as an ambassador in delivering the message of a king. If he be telling of that which by Faith he has heard and seen, and his hands have handled, of the Word of Life—if he not only believe in his utmost soul the truths he utters, but would be ready, if need were, to die for them—then his heart should not beat one throb the faster, though, like the Apostles of old, he were standing before Philosophers at Athens or Emperors at Rome. But the case of one who stands here and in this office, of one who has rather to argue than to apply, rather to defend than to enforce, is not the same. The transcendent majesty and unutterable value of the truths which he maintains—the oppressive sense of his own insufficiency—the knowledge that many far better and wiser and more learned than himself have been his predecessors, and that many far better and wiser and more learned than himself will listen to his words—all these considerations may well paralyse his energy and chill his heart. And yet if he have no other aim than to give a manly reason for the truth that is in him; if, with single-hearted simplicity, he strive to set forth some one fragment at least [1] of those arguments which have wrought in his own soul the strength of its convictions and the security of its hopes, then he may at once take courage. Happy he who, in an age which has been described as "destitute of faith yet terrified at scepticism," can still say *Manet immota Fides;* happier still is he, to whom, "having the witness in himself[2]," may be given the high grace of labouring to strengthen the faith of others. And if, after well-nigh two thousand years of apologetic literature, but little room for originality be left, on the other hand the arguments of those two millenniums have established the truth upon a more impregnable foundation[3]; if the lapse of centuries have dimmed for us the historic brightness of the facts of our religion, they have at least attested the permanence and

[1] See Appendix A.

[2] 1 John v. 10, τὴν μαρτυρίαν. 2 Cor. i. 22, ὁ καὶ σφραγισάμενος ἡμᾶς καὶ δοὺς τὸν ἀρραβῶνα τοῦ πνεύματος ἐν ταῖς καρδίαις ἡμῶν.

[3] It seems no exaggeration to say that our evidence for the truth of Christianity is at least as strong as that of the earliest disciples. To minds not yet familiar with the methods of God's working, the fearful apparent disproportion between the short period of our Lord's ministry, and the apparent insignificance of its immediate visible results when compared with His Divine claims, would have gone far to outweigh a faith founded on His miracles in an age when miracles were comparatively disregarded.

the beneficence of the system which rests upon them as its base. And since, undeniably, the rock on which Christ built His Church *has* risen unshaken out of the stormiest waves of past assault, we may well feel an undaunted confidence, that even amid the decuman billows of modern scepticism it shall remain immovable as the granite bases of the world. It may be deluged again and again by the fiercely recurrent surge,—it may be hidden again and again from the eyes of the multitude by the blinding spray,—but it is there; and so long as the feet of the Church militant on earth be planted firm upon that living rock, she may indeed be desolate, she may be wounded, she may be oppressed, but so long we believe and are sure that "the gates of Hell shall not prevail against her[1]."

It was the direction of the pious founder of these lectures[2] that they should deal with recent attacks upon

[1] Matt. xvi. 18.
[2] John Hulse, born 1708, educated at Congleton Grammar School, entered St. John's College, Cambridge, at the age of 16. Owing to ill-treatment by his father, he was mainly supported by his college. He was ordained in 1732, and was for many years curate at Gostry. On the death of his father in 1753 he succeeded to the family estate, Elworth Hall, where he lived in retirement till his death in 1790. See Memoir of Hulse in Mr. Parkinson's *Hulsean Lectures*, 1838. In Mr. Hulse's will he stated that the object of the Hulsean Lecturer should be "*to demonstrate in the most convincing and persuasive manner the truth and excellence of Christianity, so as to include not only the prophecies and miracles general and particular, but also any other proper or useful arguments, whether the same be direct or collateral proofs of the Christian religion, which he may think fittest to discourse upon,...or else any particular argument or branch thereof, and chiefly against notorious infidels whether Atheists or Deists.*" And he wished

the faith of Christians. In his day such attacks were sufficiently rare to be easily distinguishable, sufficiently definite to be separately resisted. It is not so now. We are, as it were, in the very focus of the storm. It is not that every now and then there is a burst of thunder and a glare of lightning; but the whole air is electric with quivering flames. And what is the point around which all the dangers of the storm converge? Not around minor questions, the mere ἀδιάφορα of Theology, the things unessential respecting which there need be only charity: but the storm now rages about the very Ark of God. It is the Divinity of Christ himself which is called in question, and we are challenged to prove that the most sacred archives of our religion are not a delusion or a lie. Nor is it any longer against this or that treatise that we must defend the most vital principles of Christian doctrine. It is against whole literatures; it is against whole philosophies; it is against the vague doubts of eminent thinkers; it is against the innumerable sneers, the repeated assumptions, the ever-varying criticisms of a powerful and intellectual press. It is impossible to deny the fact, it is useless to deplore it. "Our duty," said Spinosa, "is neither to ridicule the affairs of men, nor to deplore, but simply to understand them." And meanwhile it may fortify us to bear in mind that of these attacks we

the following clause to be added by way of preface to the printed Lectures. "And may the Divine blessing for ever go along with all my benefactions, and may the Greatest and Best of Beings by His all-wise Providence and gracious influence make the same effectual to His own glory and the good of my fellow-creatures."

were from the first forewarned. "This child is set for a sign which shall be spoken against[1]," said the aged Simeon as he pressed the yet infant Saviour to his heart. His cross from the first was to the Jews a stumblingblock, and to the Greeks foolishness; His earliest Apostles were denounced as "pestilent fellows and ringleaders of sedition[2];" His Gospel was stigmatised by haughty historians as an "*exitiabilis superstitio*[3]," and His self-denying children in their purest and sweetest days were distinguished by this fact only, that "everywhere they were spoken against[4]."

Eighteen hundred years have passed away, and, side by side with a happy awakenment to life and energy, we cannot deny that there is a wide-spread

---

[1] Luke ii. 34.

[2] Acts xxiv. 5, λοιμὸν καὶ κινοῦντα στάσιν. 1 Cor. iv. 13, ὡς περικαθάρματα τοῦ κόσμου ἐγενήθημεν, πάντων περίψημα.

[3] See Tac. *Ann*. XV. 44, "quos *per flagitia invisos* vulgus Christianos appellabat...repressaque in præsens *exitiabilis superstitio* rursum crumpebat, non modo per Judæam, originem *ejus mali*, sed per urbem etiam, quo cuncta undique *atrocia* aut *pudenda* confluunt." Cf. Sueton. *Ner*. 16, *Claud*. 25. Plin. *Epp*. x. 97, "Nihil aliud inveni quam *superstitionem pravam et immodicam*."

[4] Acts xxviii. 22; 1 Pet. ii. 12, iv. 14. In the expression "odio humani generis convicti" (Tac. *l.c.*), the genitive is objective, "their hatred *for* the human race." The Christians were confounded with the Jews, and their absence from the games, &c., was construed as being mere moroseness. Cf. Tac. *Hist*. V. 5, where he says "*adversus omnes alios hostile odium.*" Among other things the Christians were constantly charged with Atheism, εἴ τις ἄθεος ἢ Χριστιανὸς ἢ Ἐπικούρειος, Luc. *Alex. Pseud*. XXXVIII. Αἶρε τοὺς ἀθέους was the cry at the martyrdom of Polycarp. Cf. Dio. Cass. LXVII. 14, "Homines deploratæ, illicitæ, ac desperatæ factionis." Cæcilius in Min. Fel. *Oct*. VIII.

defection from the faith which our fathers held; nor does it require much insight to recognise that the causes of this falling away are both moral and intellectual. To enter briefly into those causes—to show that neither Philosophy nor Criticism has shaken one truth of Christianity—to show the extent and the glory of its individual, social and political victories, and thus to demonstrate the mighty Witness borne by History to the faith of Christ—will be the object of these Lectures; and I pray that with all their feebleness and imperfections they may be blessed by His Holy Spirit to the brightening of our hopes, and the deepening of our charity, by the establishment and the increase of our faith in the Son of God.

Now in attributing the spread of disbelief in part to moral causes I would at the outset, and with deep sincerity and earnestness, guard myself against a misconception. It has been a common, and I may add a deplorable mistake among Christian controversialists, to *assume* that error in the judgment must necessarily be caused by depravity in the heart. Nothing has led to deeper irritation, or more directly tended to harden into an antichristian attitude the minds of men who might have been won by less ungenerous arguments, than this endeavour to suppress free inquiry under the crushing and insulting charge of moral obliquity. To silence a doubt, or slur a difference under the uncharitable haughtiness of "*we know that this man is a sinner*[1]," is a mixture of religious Pharisaism with social

[1] John ix. 24.

impertinence[1]; and it is least of all excusable in an age which has seen a doubtful or even an adverse position towards the truth of our religion maintained by men who have deepened our love for all that is great in conduct and pure in thought, and who in their stainless lives and noble utterance give the unconscious testimony of "minds naturally Christian[2]." But while we utterly condemn in religious controversy the mixture of moral innuendo with intellectual proof, we are justified, as a warning to our own hearts no less than those of others, in asserting the undeniable truth that sometimes, though not necessarily, and in some instances, though not in all, the first rills of heresy *have* flowed from the bitter fountains of a perverse will or a corrupted heart. It remains as true now as in the days of the Apostles that "the natural man receiveth not the things of the Spirit of God[3]," and that "spiritual things must be

---

[1] In a remarkable little book called *The Modern Buddhist*, translated by Mr. Alabaster from the *Kitchanukit* of Chao Phya Ipipakon, foreign minister in Siam, we constantly find such complaints as the following, in answer to perfectly honest doubts and remarks: "*When I had said this the missionary became angry, and saying, I was hard to teach, left me.*" "The Missionary replied, '*If any one spoke like this in European countries he would be put in prison.*'" And in reply to a question as to the doctrine of original sin, "the Missionary answered, '*It is waste of time to converse with evil men who will not be taught,*' and so left me;" pp. 29, 34, 35. This, it need hardly be said, was not St. Paul's method, but the very reverse of it.

[2] "O testimonium animæ naturaliter Christianæ!" Tert. *Apolog.* 17.

[3] 1 Cor. ii. 14, *ad fin.*, &c. "How *can* ye believe which receive honour from men, and seek not the honour which cometh of God

spiritually discerned." The voice from heaven saying "This is my beloved Son" sounded to most of those who heard it but as the dull roll of the thunder; to some only as the unintelligible voice of an angel; to very few as the distinct and articulate utterance of God [1]. If it was a Christian historian who took for his motto "*Pectus est quod facit theologum* [2]," it was a sceptical poet [3] who wrote, "*As are the inclinations so are the opinions*," it was an idealising philosopher who said "*that our system of thought was often only the history of our heart* [4]." Oh my brethren, we may lose our faith in Christ from many causes, and from some which it is not for fallible man to denounce or to condemn; but it is well for us to know there is undoubtedly one path which leads with dangerous frequency from prac-

---

only?" John v. 44. Compare such passages as Ps. xxv. 14; John vii. 17; Rom. viii. 7, xiv. 17, &c. "Il y a assez de lumière pour ceux qui ne désirent que de voir, et assez d'obscurité pour ceux qui ont une disposition contraire." Pascal, *Pensées*, II. 151, ed. Faugère. "Christian faith," says an American writer of genius, "is a grand cathedral with divinely-pictured windows. Standing *without*, you see no glory nor can possibly imagine any: standing *within*, each ray of light reveals a harmony of unspeakable splendour." Nath. Hawthorne, *Transformation*, p. 262.

[1] ὁ μὲν ἔχων τὰ κρείττονα ὦτα ἀκούει Θεοῦ· ὁ δὲ κεκωφωμένος τὴν τῆς ψυχῆς ἀκοὴν ἀναισθητεῖ λέγοντος Θεοῦ. Orig. c. *Cels*. II. 72.

[2] Neander. Hence the nickname *Pectoralisten* given to his followers.

[3] Göthe.

[4] Fichte, *Unser Denksystem ist sehr oft nur die Geschichte unseres Herzens*. Similarly he says that "Truth is descended from conscience," and that "men do not will according to their reason, but reason according to their will." *Bestimmung der Menschen*, p. 293, &c.

tical faithlessness to speculative infidelity; from the
"Yea, hath God said?" to the "Ye shall not surely
die [1]." Let us then at least beware that in us unholiness
do not cloud the spiritual eye and dull the spiritual
ear: for the rank mists which reek upward from the
sinful heart *do* tend most fatally to obliterate the Image,
the Memory, the Life of Christ—they end by hiding
from the human soul even the vision of its Creator
in fold on fold of a more and more impenetrable
night [2].

[1] Cf. Pascal, *Pens.* II. 108, "Nous connaissons la vérité non
seulement par la raison, mais encore par le cœur." "Love God
and He will dwell with you; obey God and He will reveal the
truth of His deepest teaching to you." Robertson, *God's Revelation:
of Heaven*. But no one has expressed this truth in nobler language
than Clem. Alex., *Strom.* V. I. 13, Καὶ τοῦτο ἦν ὃ ᾐνίξατο ὅστις ἄρα
ἦν ἐκεῖνος ὃ ἐπίγραψας τῇ εἰσόδῳ τοῦ ἐν Ἐπιδαύρῳ νεῷ·
  ἁγνὸν χρὴ νήοιο θυώδεος ἐντὸς ἰόντα
  ἔμμεναι· ἁγνείη δ' ἔστι φρονεῖν ὅσια—
and then, after quoting Matt. xviii. 3, he continues, ἐνταῦθα γάρ ὁ
νεὼς τοῦ Θεοῦ τρισὶν ἡδρασμένος θεμελίοις, πίστει, ἐλπίδι, ἀγάπῃ φαί-
νεται. Cf. id. VII. X. 57. A crowd of writers in all ages have
testified to the same fact. " *Teneritas conscientiæ*," says Tertullian,
"*obduratur in callositatem voluntarii erroris*." *Ad Nationes*, II. I.
Shakspeare has not suffered it to pass unnoticed:
  "For when we in our viciousness grow hard,
  Oh misery on't, the wise gods seal our eyes,
  In our own filth drop our clear judgments, make us
  Adore our errors, laugh at us while we strut
  To our confusion."
" *Wer es glaubt, dem ist das Heilge nach,*" said Schiller; and so too
Schleiermacher, "*Der Glaube ist in mir lebendig durch die That.*"
[2] Witness the historic filiation of such writers as La Mettraie to
Voltaire; of Strauss to Hegel, and of Feuerbach and Bruno Bauer to

In speaking, however, of the moral causes for prevalent disbelief, I am not alluding at all to single cases, but to that subtler, more indefinable, more general something which we may call the Spirit of the Age. If pride and fashion have often been fatal conspirators against individual faith, so have wider but more specious evils wrought a certain atrophy in the spiritual life of nations and centuries. Ages of the most advanced refinement have not unfrequently been ages of the most open unbelief[1]. At the zenith of their civilization nations have often been at the nadir of their faith[2]. There has been on absorbing luxury, and luxury makes the heart soft,

Strauss. In the old philosophy we may notice the same kind of downward progress, from Protagoras to Diagoras of Melos.

[1] "In the perplexities of nations, in their struggles for existence, their infancy, their impotence, or even their disorganization, they have higher hopes and nobler passions: out of the suffering comes the serious mind; out of the salvation, the grateful heart; out of endurance, fortitude; out of deliverance, faith...But when they have done away with violent and external sources of suffering, worse evils seem to arise out of their rest; evils that vex less and mortify more, that suck the blood though they do not shed it, and ossify the heart though they do not torture it." Ruskin's *Mod. Painters*, II. 5. The whole of the noble passage of which this is an extract is well worthy of study.

[2] Bacon, in his Essay "*Of Atheisme*," after saying that "None deny there is a God, but those for whom it maketh that there were no God," adds among the causes of Atheism "*Learned Times*, specially with Peace and Prosperity: for troubles and adversity doe more bow men's mindes to Religion." *Ess.* XVI. "L'abus du savoir produit l'incrédulité. Tout savant dédaigne le sentiment vulgaire; chacun en veut avoir un à soi. L'orgueilleuse philosophie mène à l'esprit fort comme l'aveugle dévotion mène au fanatisme." Rousseau. (This and other passages from Rousseau I quote from

and effeminate, and vulnerable : there has been an eager race for wealth, and the love of wealth deadens all the soul's finer sensibilities; there have been unbounded means of gratification, and selfish pleasure makes men earthly, and cruel, and coarse. Entangled in complex interests, amused by incessant frivolities, stimulated by restless excitements, beguiled by the dazzling treacheries of a refined immorality, for such ages the horizon of life has dwindled into an ever-narrowing circle, and amid the dust and glare of material interests, all heavenly hopes, all Godward aspirations have faded utterly away. The spectacle is full of warning for ourselves. It shows us that material advance may be moral retrogression, and that widely-extended comfort, rapidly-increasing knowledge, vast literary activity may co-exist in Philosophy with a dreary materialism, in morals with a corrupted selfishness, in religion with a blank negation. It proves to us—and at this moment the white cliffs of England seem to reverberate to us in echoing thunder the solemn lesson—it proves to us that not on refinement, but on spirituality; not on selfishness, but on sacrifice; not on knowledge, but on wisdom; not on intelligence, but on faith, rests the entire superstructure of national greatness and individual peace. Is it a true philosophy which prides itself on a perfect impartiality between the faith which in the fifteenth century produced a

---

Pensées et Maximes de J. J. Rousseau.) *Œuvres Complètes*, Vol. XXXVI. p. 45.

Picus of Mirandola, and in the eighteenth a Vincent
de Paul, and that immoral deism which culminated
in the one century in an Aretino and a Poggio, and in
the other in a Marât and a Robespierre [1]? My brethren,
let us beware lest, while the censer is in our hands,
the spot of leprosy be on our foreheads. There is but
one direction in which the disease can be developed;
there is but one remedy whereby it can be cleansed.

To these moral causes for the growth of unbelief
it will be needless to return; our task summons us to
deal with those which are more purely intellectual, and
have their seat in the understanding rather than in the
heart. There are assaults upon Christianity which have
their ground in philosophy, in science, and in historical
criticism. It is not easy to encounter them because once,
like the tents of the nomads, they were shifted from
day to day, but now the very frequency of their intru-
sion has won for them, among too many, the position
of scattered indeed yet tolerated settlers. So that now
it seems as though against the doctrines, and above all
against the miracles of Christianity, there were, so to
speak, "a conspiracy of silence," an agreement of con-

---

[1] I borrow the expression from De Lammenais, *Ess. sur l'Indifférence en Matières de Religion*, 1. 250. "*On s'enorgueillit de garder
la neutralité de l'ignorance entre la doctrine qui a produit Vincent de
Paul et celle qui a produit Marât.*" Giovanni Pico della Mirandola
(*b.* 1463, *d.* 1491) after his early period of exuberant display may
certainly be regarded as one of the most sincere and interesting
characters of the fifteenth century. Aretino, one of the vainest and
vilest of men, belongs in point of time rather to the 16th century,
having been born in 1491.

temptuous indifference; as though forsooth it were too late in the day to argue or to refute, and it were at once more effectual and more courteous to ignore. For instance, the central doctrine of Christianity is based upon a miracle, and in no small realm of literature the impossibility of miracles is calmly insisted upon as a discovery which needs no demonstration. Their invention is attributed to an imaginative reverence; their reception to an ignorant credulity; the present belief in them to the cant of an interested hypocrisy, or the deficiencies of intellectual gifts [1]. And are we timidly to admit these haughty assertions? are we meekly to bow before the intolerant dogmatism of an ignorant science? are we, the successors of those who overcame

[1] Can anything be more insolent than the language used by Strauss on this subject? He says "It certainly required *no small amount of assurance* for any one to stand forth in the face of the present age *with an ostensibly sincere profession of implicit belief in miracle*...When Gfrörer declares in relation to the treating of the cripple &c. that he regards these cases simply as miraculous, this we understand as *a slap in the face administered to the scepticism of the philosophical critic*, or as a *thump upon the taproom table on which he made his peroration*; but we know how little he is in earnest from the way in which he contrives to set aside other miracles." *New Life of Jesus* (*Authorised Transl.* I. 38, 39). A little further on he says that Meyer's acquiescence in the Gospel narratives as miraculous "becomes in this instance *an admission of his own imbecility;*" and that Ebrard's views upon this subject "bespeak *the consummate insolence of orthodox reaction;*" and that (p. 42) the "pompous and stunning phraseology" of Ewald "sounds like a portentous sign of that last stage of existence in which the whole of this style of theology may be said to be awaiting its doom." This is a style of invective to which we hope that theologians will never, under any provocation, condescend to recur.

the world, to accept the patronising condescension which is willing to spare our venerable prejudices? Nay, unshaken amid the storm of contemptuous assertion, we reply that it requires a loftier height of intelligence to believe in miracles than to reject them [1], because it involves the realisation of loftier than mere material verities, and the recognition of wider than purely physical laws. And can it, we ask, be so decisive a sign of contemptible inferiority, to hold a faith which was dear to the heart and acceptable to the intellect, I will not say of a Milton only, or a Bossuet, but of philosophers and mathematicians, of biologists and astronomers, of a Leibnitz and a Descartes, of a Haller and a Pascal, of a Copernicus and a Kepler, of a Bacon and a Ray [2]? Have we in the last century discovered laws so far more general than the law of gravitation, that the belief in Prophecy and Miracle which

---

[1] See Grau, *Ueber den Glauben als die höchste Vernunft*, 1865. "Nur wenige Menschen sind weise genug anzusehen, dass es viel mehr Geist dazu braucht, um Wunder zu glauben, als Verstand um sie zu leugnen." Schenkel, *Was ist Wahrheit?* p. 20.

[2] See a crowd of such testimonies quoted from Ritter, Agassiz, Martius, Newton, Kepler, &c. in Uhlhorn, *Die modernen Darstellungen des Lebens Jesu*, pp. 143 sqq. For some account of the calm and simple piety of Euler and Haller, see Hagenbach, *Germ. Rationalism*, pp. 112—115 (*Engl. Tr.*). The epitaph of Copernicus is well known:

"Non parem Pauli gratiam requiro,
 Veniam Petri neque posco; sed quam
 In crucis ligno dederas latroni
  Sedulus oro."

"It is true that a little Philosophy inclineth a man's minde to was natural to a Newton should be so drivelling in us? And with so many supreme intellects still among us, so many over whom the grave has but recently closed, who have humbly held our faith in all its breadth and in all its simplicity, are we to regard the days as past in which

"Piety has found
Friends in the friends of science, and true prayer
Has flown from lips wet with Castalian dews?"

Nay, but beside the graves of a Whewell and a Faraday let all at least that is shallow and noisy in modern Atheism, learn the humility of science, and the calm dignity of unshaken Christian faith!

If we seek, my brethren, for the causes of this rejection of the supernatural, we shall find them partly in the recent tendency of metaphysical speculation, partly in certain logical inferences, partly in the increasing strength of various scientific conceptions; and each of these, as briefly as possible, we will consider in order.

I. However noble may have been the lives of Spinoza, Kant, Fichte, Schelling, Hegel, and their lives were very noble; however sincerely they may have claimed—and most of them did claim—the position

Atheisme; But depth in Philosophy bringeth men's mindes about to Religion: *For while the minde of man looketh upon Secona Causes scattered*, it may sometimes rest in them, and goe no further: But when it beholdeth the chaine of them confederate and linked together, it must needs flie to Providence and Deitie." Bacon, Essay XVI. *Of Atheisme*. The same thought is repeatedly to be found in Pascal. See Luthardt, *Apolog. Vort.* 262.

F. H. L. 2

of humble Christians[1] and religious philosophers; however magnificently they may have asserted—and some of them did assert with unequalled force—the majesty of the moral law within; above all, however little it may be fitting for us to pass judgment upon men so good and wise, with intolerant bigotry or austere condemnation,—yet certainly the total effect of their speculations was to idealise, say rather, to evaporate the facts of Christianity[2],—to substitute the supposed intuitions of a

---

[1] Cicero had said "Eos qui philosophiæ operam dant, non arbitrari Deos esse." *De Invent.* I. 29. But there is happily the distinctest evidence that Kant, Schelling, Fichte, Jacobi, Hegel were sincere Christians, although many passages of their philosophical writings undoubtedly tended to a mere idealization of Christian truths. See Hagenbach, *Germ. Rationalism*, 296, 317, 405, Engl. Tr.

[2] Kant used indignantly to repel every word spoken in disparagement of the historic Saviour, and said that he bowed reverently before His name, and regarding himself in comparison as a bungler interpreting Him as best he could (Vorowski's *Life of Kant*, p. 86, n.), yet no doubt the immediate effects of his system "were to destroy revelation by leaving nothing to be revealed" (Rev. A. S. Farrar, *Bampton Lect.* p. 323). For Schelling's views, see *Methode des Akad. Studium, Vorles.* 9. In his old age, however, as Heine scornfully says of him, "dieser Mann est abtrünnig geworden von seiner eignen Lehre...er ist zurückgeschlichen in den Glaubenstall der Vergangenheit." *Salon*, p. 275. That Strauss is the natural development of Hegel, see his *Glaubenslehre*, II. 214, *Die Halben und die Ganzen*, p. 42, "Ich machte meine Sache so gut als ich auf meinem damaligen Standpunkte könnte. *Dieser Standpunkt war der der Hegel'schen Philosophie*," &c. Feuerbach again is the natural successor of Strauss, who in his *Christian Märklin* thanks him for "das Pünktchen das er auf unser I gesetzt." "Feuerbach, will ich jetzt sagen, hat das Doppeljoch, wohin bei Hegel Philosophie und Theologie noch gingen, zerbrochen." *Die Halb. und die Ganzen*, p. 50. See too

natural[1] for the firm truths of a revealed religion[2]. In their hands the simple faith in Christ was sublimated into a mere religious Theosophy, and the doctrine of His divinity furtively relegated from the light of history into a misty region of intellectual subtleties.

And though understood only by the few, yet the effect of these systems extended to the many; and some who would have been unable to comprehend a single step of the arguments on which such views are founded, have yet grown to regard God as a "mere form of thought," and the belief in His objective existence as an imbecility of the understanding. Now we must not only admit,

---

Schwartz, *Gesch. d. Neuest. Theol.* p. 24. Fichte says "Nur das Metaphysische keineswegs aber das Historische, macht selig; das letztere macht nur verständig." Hegel expressed similar opinions, *Phänomenologie*, pp. 568, 572, 574. *Gesch. d. Philosophie*, III. 249. From Chalybäus, *Historical Survey of Speculative Philosophy* (translated by Mr Tulke), from Mansel's *Metaphysics*, 299 sqq. 302—320, or from Mr G. H. Lewes's brilliant *Biog. Hist. of Philosophy*, vol. II., the English reader may gain a fair general conception of the views of Kant, Fichte, Schelling, and Hegel. Even the slightest adequate survey of their views will be sufficient to establish the proof of what is said in the text.

[1] "La religion naturelle n'existe que dans les livres." Guizot, *Méditations*, II. 137.

[2] "The Infinite and the Absolute are names of *two counter imbecilities of the human mind* transported into properties of the nature of things; subjective negatives converted into objective affirmations." Sir W. Hamilton. "Fichte is compelled to confess that he knows no other God than the moral order of things." Mansel, *Metaph.* p. 306. "In its consequences the Philosophy of the Absolute admits of no alternative but Atheism or Pantheism...*Religion is equally annihilated under both suppositions;* for if there is no God, whom are we to worship? and if all things are God, who is to worship Him?

but it may even prove to us a source of fresh insight if we admit, that we cannot as arguments refute many of the arguments of the Idealist Philosophy; that it *may* be logically proved that Time, and Space, and Cause, are but forms of the conditioned; that they are conceivable only as negations; that all our conceptions of primary, no less than of secondary qualities, are essentially subjective, and that their synthesis in an imaginary substance is purely mental[1]. And doubtless on these logical concessions some startling conclusions might be built. But what is the result of all these concessions? Simply this, that we reject the entire reasoning on which they are founded as unpractical and trivial, and refuse to be led into a quaking fen of infidelity by the mere *ignes fatui* of metaphysical speculation[2]. It was Hume himself who

---

Morality is equally annihilated under both suppositions; for if I am the Absolute [*Fichte*], I create my own moral duties, and cannot be required to conform to any standard independent of myself; and if I am a mode of the Divine Being [*Hegel, Schelling*], my actions flow from the self-determinations of the Deity, and are all equally necessary and equally Divine." *Id.* p. 322.

[1] "We live once and for all in relations, and need nothing further." Herbart, *Allgem. Metaph.* II. 414. The logical proof of this is given with admirable force and lucidity in Prof. Ferrier's *Institutes of Metaphysics*. Yet in reading such books, with the highest admiration for their intellectual power, one is sometimes reminded of Göthe's words:

" Ein Kerl, der speculirt,
  Ist wie ein Vieh, auf dürrer Heide
  Von einem bösen Geist herumgeführt,
  Und rings umher ist grüne Weide."

[2] " Que si vos facultés vibrant simultanément n'ont jamais rendu ce grand son unique que nous appelons Dieu, je n'ai rien plus à dire;

said of such arguments that "they admit of no answer and produce no conviction." What is denied to us as an axiom we claim as a postulate; what is refused as a deduction we assume as an intuition; if such trains of thought be true for the understanding, we repudiate them for the reason; if they be logically impregnable, we declare them to be spiritually false. We look at the rainbow, and Kant, by a process of reasoning of the most delicate and subtle character, proves to us with irresistible conviction that the colours, and the clouds, and the sun, and the falling rain, are but subjective conceptions—are but mere modifications of the Ego having no relation to anything real which may remain; nay, more, that the very time of their falling and the space in which they move, are but innate forms of the understanding[1]; and yet

---

vous manquez de l'élément essentiel et caracteristique de notre nature." Renan, *Et. d'Hist. Rel.* p. 418. These metaphysical inquiries may, however, have a salutary effect in checking the "fatal ingenuity of the theologians," and in showing the futility of an idle dogmatism on subjects of such abysmal difficulty as the περιχώρησις, the τρόπος ἀντιδόσεως, the συνάφεια, the χρῆσις τῆς κτίσεως and κένωσις τῆς χρήσεως, and all those "parts of the ancient dogmatic system which may be allowed silently to fall into disuse as beyond the proper range of human thought and human language." Milman, *Latin Christianity*, VI. 634. Abundant evidence of this "fatal ingenuity," may be seen in Oischinger, *Die Christliche und Scholastische Theologie*, Jan. 1869, or in Dorner's celebrated work on the Person of Christ.

[1] "In the rainbow we shall indeed, according to the ordinary mode of representation, first of all call the coloured arch a phenomenon present merely for us and for our visible sense, but shall regard the rain-drops as the actual and true thing in itself that lies at the bottom of this phenomenon. But let us now consider that these

knowing all this and admitting it[1], as a play of reasoning, to be unanswerable, we yet gaze on the rainbow shining there in its sevenfold perfection of divided light, and we shall not only be undisturbed by its possessing a merely subjective reality, but even more than this, we shall accept it still as a symbol of mercy to a sinful and stormy world, and shall joyfully recall that prophecy of redemption, "the rainbow round about the throne in sight like unto an emerald[2]." As the Predestinarian may prove to us that we are but puppets of the divine will,—clay foredoomed to dishonour by the potter's hands,—but we shall still act as though we were absolutely free; even so when sceptical philosophies have shattered the arguments from final causes, and tried to demonstrate to us that neither from Scripture, nor from any primary intuition, can we be sure of so much as the existence of

---

drops again, are only empiric phenomena, and then *their round form, nay, even the space in which they are formed*, are nothing in themselves but a mere modification or principle of our sensuous intuition; with all this, however, the object itself remains to us completely unknown." Kant, *Kritik der Reinen Vernunft*, p. 45, quoted by Chalybäus.

[1] As even Dr. Brown, the great opponent of Idealism, frankly admits. We may say of metaphysical formulæ and symbols, as Prof. Huxley does of materialistic, that when they are taken for anything but formulæ and symbols, they may "paralyse the energy and destroy the beauty of a life." *Lay Sermons*, p. 161. For instance, "the two Hegelian conclusions, that God is personal only in man, and the soul immortal only in God, clearly imply that neither is God personal, nor the soul immortal." Janet, *Materialism*, p. 5 (tr. Masson). Views like these led by a natural sequence of thought to the autolatry of Max Stirner with its motto, *Quisque sibi Deus*.

[2] Rev. iv. 3.

a God, we still simply refuse to be tormented from our unshaken belief by the destructive ingenuity of our own logic; we quietly ignore these Antinomies of Reason, and after listening to Spinoza telling us that "to speak of God's assuming human nature is as absurd as if we said that a circle had taken the nature of a square;" still, in a spirit as invincibly calm as the *credo quia impossibile* of the ancient Father, we kneel humbly on our knees, and with eyes and hands upraised to heaven, pray to that phantasmal Deity who they tell us is but an idol of our own fancy,—pray to Him not as to a mere *anima mundi* or cosmic life, not as to a mere transmutation of matter[1], not as to a mere "category of the ideal," least of all, for the sake of some reflex action upon ourselves— but *pray to Him as to a living God and merciful Father;* knowing by the earnest of the Spirit, knowing by a witness within ourselves, that we shall receive from Him, through His Eternal and Incarnate Son, those daily miracles in the very possibility of which they tell us it is an imbecility to have believed[2].

[1] Moleschott, who with Büchner and Karl Vogt represents the most advanced school of Materialism, talks of the *Allgewalt des Stoffwechsels*. "Der Gott Straussens ist der Naturgesetz; der Gott Hegels ist der Begriff; der Gott Feuerbachs ist der illusorische Doppelgänger der Menschen; der Gott Moleschotts ist die Materie. Nachdem diese Götter, die Gebilde den Menschenwitzes und des Menschenwahns, sich...in der Dämmerung der grauen Theorie todtgeschlagen haben, darf auch ich den Wunsch hegen, dass...das Morgenroth der Erlösung tagen möge?" Hafermann, *Athen oder Bethlehem?* p. 125.

[2] πάντες δὲ θεῶν χατέουσ' ἄνθρωποι. Hom. *Od.* III. 48. "Deus non est Æternitas vel Infinitas sed æternus et infinitus: non est Duratio vel Spatium sed durat et adest." Sir I. Newton. "J'aime Dieu,

II. Nor are we surprised that metaphysicians themselves should have shrunk back appalled from their own conclusions, and found themselves compelled to rebuild in the region of practical belief what they had demolished in that of philosophical knowledge [1]. But the rejection

---

je n'aime pas l'être suprême," said a man of genius, Bungener, *Vol'aire et ses Temps*, p. 241. Compare the admirably truthful and honest remarks of Niebuhr, "As for that Christianity which is such according to the fashion of modern philosophers and Pantheists, without a personal God, without immortality......it may be a very ingenious and subtle philosophy, but it is no Christianity at all. Again and again have I said that *I know not what to do with a metaphysical God*, and that I will have no other but the God of the Bible who is *heart* and *heart*. Whoever can reconcile the metaphysical God with the God of the Bible may try it...but he who admits the absolute inexplicability of the main point which can only be approached by asymptotes, will never grieve at the impossibility of possessing any *system* of religion." *Leben Niebuhr's*, II. 344. "On my way I found the God of the Pantheists, but I could make nothing of him. This poor visionary creature is interwoven with, and grown into the world, indeed is almost imprisoned in it, and yawns at you, without voice, without power. To have will one must have personality, and to manifest oneself, one must have elbow-room." Heine (quoted *Trench on Miracles*, p. 71, 9th ed.). Claudius compared an ideal relation without personality, to a painted horse which you can admire but not ride. Jacobi wanted to know nothing of a God who made the eye but does not see, the ear but does not hear, the understanding but neither knows, nor wills, and therefore *is* not. Hagenbach, *Germ. Rat.* pp. 296, 298.

[1] Chalybäus, *Speculative Philosophy*, Eng. Tr. p. 49. Strauss, *Leben Jesu*, III. p. 144, seems aghast at the results of his own criticism, and endeavours "to re-establish dogmatically, what has been destroyed critically." The best account of the manner in which Fichte, Schelling, Hegel, &c. reconciled their theories with the objective historical existence of Christ, may be found in Dorner's *Entwickelungsgesch. der Lehre der Person Christi.*

of the supernatural is due also in no small degree to direct and often-repeated arguments founded on the alleged inadequacy of all testimony and immutability of all laws. And before dealing with these let us understand that the issue before us is distinct and definite. However skilfully the modern ingenuity of semi-belief may have tampered with supernatural interpositions, it is clear to every honest and unsophisticated mind that, if miracles be incredible, Christianity is false. If Christ wrought no miracles then the gospels are untrustworthy; if Christ rose not, which is a stupendous miracle—then is our preaching vain, and your faith is vain, and ye are yet in your sins, and we are found liars to God, and they—however desolate, however heartrending the belief—they that are fallen asleep in Christ are perished[1]. If the Resurrection be merely a spiritual idea, or a mythicised hallucination, then our religion has been founded on an error and a sham. We accept the issue. Eliminate miracles, and then though there still remain a moral system singularly noble and singularly pure—yet it is a moral Deism alone. A Christianity without its Redeemer, without its sanctions, without its hopes—a Christianity dissevered from the promises of the future and the history of the past—a Christianity based on

[1] 1 Cor. xv. 18. The last prayer of Thistlewood, the Cato Street conspirator, "O God, if there be a God, save my soul, if I have a soul," rings with the echoes of an intense despair; but it is an abyss far lower than this to affirm dogmatically that there is no soul, no salvation, and no immortality. Strauss ends his *Glaubenslehre* with the remark that the belief in a future life is the *last enemy* (!) which speculative criticism has to overcome.

the credulity of superstitions, and disseminated by the potency of lies, is not the Christianity of our convictions, not a Christianity for which we care to retain the name. If it be true that the growth of science and civilisation are incompatible with a belief in the miraculous, then must science and civilisation listen for the voice of some new deliverer, for then Christianity is dead [1].

i. Now as regards the inadequacy of testimony to establish a miracle, modern scepticism has not advanced one single step beyond the blank assertion. And it is astonishing that this assertion should still be considered cogent, when its logical consistency has been shattered to pieces by a host of writers as well sceptical as Christian [2]. For, as the greatest of our living logicians has remarked, the supposed recondite and dangerous formula of Hume —that it is more probable that testimony should be mistaken than that miracles should be true—reduces itself to the very harmless proposition that anything is incre-

---

[1] "Strauss hat ganz Recht wenn er die Wunderfrage als *die Existenzfrage des Christenthums* behandelt." Uhlhorn, *Die Mod. Darstell. des Lebens Jesu*, p. 106.

[2] Mill's *Logic*, II. 157—160. Dr Whewell points out most clearly that in Inductive inferences a new element is added to the combination of facts, "a conception of the mind is superinduced on the general proposition which did not exist in the observed facts." In fact, as Mr. Mill says, this kind of Induction is "merely a shorthand registration of the facts known," and not an inference from facts known to facts unknown. "Induction," to use Dr Whewell's metaphor, "moves upwards and Deduction downwards, on the same stair, but they move differently. Deduction descends steadily and methodically step by step ; Induction mounts by a leap beyond the reach of method, and bounds to the top of the stair."

dible which is contrary to a complete induction. It is in fact a flagrant petitio principii, used to support a wholly unphilosophical assertion. As regards the petitio principii, we shall meet it hereafter by testing the cogency of the Christian evidences; as regards the assertion that *no* amount of evidence could establish the supernatural, we ask in amazement on what it is philosophically based? Does it rest on anything higher than the idle habit of mind induced by the observation of constant recurrences? Is it anything more than the intensified essence of the old faithless question, " Where is the promise of His coming? for since the fathers fell asleep, all things continue as they were from the beginning of the creation[1]." Even were the induction on which it is founded an exhaustive one, so far from producing any conviction, it would, as Bishop Butler pointed out more than 100 years ago, merely prove the commonplace truism, that it is probable that things should continue as they are, except in cases in which there is reason to think that they will be changed. In fact the Inductive process cannot prove absolute conclusions; the first stage of it, as has been well said, is not reasoning but observation; the second is not reasoning but instinct. Under the best of circumstances it can only be used to establish an universal by thrusting imagination into the province of logic[2]. When used to deny the possibility

[1] 2 Pet. iii. 4; cf. Luke xii. 45; Is. v. 19. "What is disturbed by a miracle is the mechanical expectation of a recurrence." Mozley, *Bampt. Lect.* p. 56.

[2] "It is very convenient to indicate that all the conditions of belief have been fulfilled in this case [gravitation] by calling the

of miracles, it is abused in identically the same way that an inhabitant of the Great Sahara might abuse it to deny the reality of snow, or as the French Academy actually did abuse it to deny the existence of meteorites. A comet moving in an hyperbolic orbit may have been visible but once during millions of terrestrial years, would it therefore be philosophical to deny its possibility? No. It has been unanswerably said that " the Inductive principle is in its very nature only an expectation. It is as radically incompetent to pronounce an universal proposition, as the taste or smell is to decide on matters of sight. Its function is practical not logical. Transmuted into an Universal, the inductive principle issues out of the metamorphosis a fiction not a truth : a weapon of air which, even in the hand of a giant, can inflict no blow, because it is itself a shadow [1]."

ii. But let us admit that the disbelief in miracles does not rest on this imperfect induction, and imaginative fallacy alone, but still more on the magnificent discovery of those general laws which have tended to impress the minds of men with a sense, not only of the order, beauty, and harmony, but also of the immutability

---

statement that unsupported stones will fall to the ground 'a law of nature.' But when, as commonly happens, we change *will* into *must*, we introduce *an idea of necessity* which assuredly does not lie in the observed facts, and has no warranty that I can discover elsewhere. For my part I utterly repudiate and anathematise the intruder. *Fact I know, and Law I know ; but what is this necessity but an empty shadow of my own mind's throwing?"* Huxley *on the Physical Basis of Life. Lay Sermons*, p. 158.

[1] Mozley, *on Miracles*, Bampton Lectures, 1865, p. 61.

of nature[1]. Spinoza asserted that God and nature were not two but one; that the laws of the latter are the will of the former in its constant realisation; and that to believe in God's doing anything against the observed order of the universe is to believe in His acting contray to His own nature[2]. Now since the days of Spinoza science has made gigantic strides, and all her discoveries have tended to obliterate apparent exceptions and anomalies, and to inspire an ardent hope that her ultimate victory will be to prove that all material phenomena are due to the working of one vast law. And hence—partly from the narrowness which has led to a suspicion of science among Christian teachers—partly from the counter narrowness which has confined the attention of physicists to some limited speciality—partly from the mutual antagonisms thus generated, and the apparent stationariness of religious thought amid the vast progress of scientific discovery—Science has grown more and more material in its conceptions, and the alleged immutability of natural laws, though it be but a mere idol of the theatre which has been promoted into an idol of the tribe, has been suffered more and more to usurp the very throne of the living God. Henceforth it seems we are to believe that the Creator has abdicated in favour of

[1] Rousseau said of the question as to the possibility of miracles, "cette question serait sérieusement traitée impie, si elle n'était pas absurde." *Lettres de la Montagne*, III. See Lange, *Leben Jesu*, II. iii. 9. Strauss, *Christl. Glaubensl.* I. 229.

[2] See Baden Powell's *Order of Nature*, and Essay in *Essays and Reviews*, which have been ably answered by Dean Mansel in *Aids to Faith*.

His own dead laws[1]; that, impotent, or else indifferent, He has withdrawn into the far depths of His own eternity; that instead of seeking Him we must henceforth only ask the sun about His wisdom, and the sea about His love; and that to pray to Him is as futile a superstition as to bid the hurricane furnish us with courage to meet our daily difficulties, to ask the pestilence to excuse our frailties, or the earthquake to forgive our sins[2]!

But after all, though we hear so much of the reign of Law, what *is* a Law[3]? Is it anything in the world beyond that act of apprehension by which, because of our limited understandings, we make "one act a phantom of succession"? Is it anything but an observation of recurrences, and a colligation of many observed recurrences under one single category which we call a cause? Even in stating it the nature of the thing defined escapes us;

---

[1] This would be indeed the "*Deus unicus, solitarius, destitutus*," which the ancient Christians were taunted with worshipping. Min. Felix, *Octav.* x. See Göthe, *Sprüche in Reimen; Werke*, III. 3.
   "Was wär ein Gott, der nur von aussen stiesse
   Im Kreis das All am Finger laufen liesse?" &c.

[2] "Relégué au fond de son éternité sourde et obscure, si nous l'interrogeons, si nous le supplions, si nous crions vers lui, il ne peut pas nous répondre, supposé toutefois qu'il puisse nous répondre, *Que voulez-vous?* J'ai fait des lois, demandez au soleil et aux étoiles, demandez à la mer et aux sables de ses rivages, pour moi mon sort est accompli, je ne suis plus rien que le repos et le serviteur contemplatif des œuvres de ma droite." Lacordaire, *Conférence*, 1846, p. 33.

[3] "Die Naturgesetze sind ein unbekanntes X: kein Mensch kennt sie, man hat von ihrem Wesen kaum eine Ahnung." Hafermann, *Athen oder Bethlehem?* p. 35.

it flies as it were with wings beyond that adamantine wall of mystery which surrounds every step we take into the region of the unseen. "That," says Hooker, "which doth assign unto each thing the kind, that which doth appoint the form and measure the working, the same we term a law." And when we talk of the Laws of Nature, do we not merely add one vagueness to another? For what is Nature? if it be not a mere reverend synonym for God, what is it but the sum total of observed phenomena,—the active powers impressed on matter by some unknown cause "brought into a form of unity for the purposes of science, and impersonated for the convenience of language¹"? It was the immortal glory of Newton to have discovered a law—perhaps even here we ought in absolute strictness to say—to have framed an hypothesis, which reduced under one set of conditions the most immense diversity of phenomena; which referred to the same cause alike the fall of a rose-leaf, nay, even of each impalpable germ in the summer air, and the inconceivable velocities of comets as they rush among the orbs of heaven. But yet what is gravitation? by what inconceivable means does one atom act upon another through intervening space? Does the term explain one whit more of the nature of the action than the terms lapidity or aureity explain of the natures of stones or gold²? Nay, the very value of the term which facilitated

---

[1] Green, *Vital Dynamics*. In point of fact the word "Nature" is but the substitution, in the metaphysical stage of the human understanding, of one unknown entity for the *many* which are supposed in the stage of Fetisch-worship.

[2] "No further insight into why the apple falls is acquired by

its introduction[1] was that it expressed a simple fact without involving any hypothesis. Surely to place mere 'relations of succession and resemblance" between ourselves and God, to imagine or to observe a connecting link in the chain of apparent causes, and then, idolising and idealising this helpless inconceivable thing, to attribute to it the physical and moral government of the universe,—is to tighten, not to lift the veil of Isis[2]; it is to blur the crystal glass of nature till it can neither transmit nor reflect the light of heaven.

And is it not amazing that this antagonism to the supernatural, this denial of the divine should come so often from the students of nature? Strange that any should disbelieve in God who have so deeply studied His works, and that *they* should deny His special interpositions who see most of His daily miracles[3]. The

---

saying it is forced to fall, or falls by the force of gravitation ; by the latter expression we are able most usefully to relate it to other phenomena ; but we still know no more of the particular phenomenon, than that under certain circumstances the apple does fall." Grove, *On the Correlation of Physical Forces*, p. 18. See Janet, *Materialism*, p. 68.

[1] Comte, *Phil. Posit.* II. iii. § 2 (in Miss Martineau's Transl. I. p. 183). "This term has every merit. It expresses a simple fact without any reference to the nature or cause of this universal action. It affords *the only explanation which positive science admits;* i.e., *the connection between certain less known facts and other better known facts.*"

[2] "Isis is the Ægypto-Greek symbol of the unconditioned. On her temple at Sais was inscribed, ἐγώ εἰμι πᾶν τὸ γεγονὸς καὶ ὂν καὶ ἐσόμενον καὶ ἐμοῦ πέπλον οὐδείς πω θνητὸς ἀπεκάλυψε." Sir W. Hamilton, *Disc. on Philosophy*, p. 22.

[3] "Quotidiana Dei miracula ex assiduitate viluerunt," Gregory,

greatest interpreters of science have ever been the humblest, because alike, " in the choir of heaven and the furniture of earth," they have recognized the immensity of human ignorance[1]. " The eternal silence of those unknown spaces fills me with dread," said Pascal; but " The heavens declare no longer the glory of God, but that of Newton and Kepler[2]," is the flippant blasphemy of modern arrogance. Kant said that two things "filled his soul with awe,—the starry heaven above and the moral law within;" but Hegel in one passage of his writings speaks of the world of stars with a studied

---

Hom. XXVI. in *Evang.* Lucret. II. 1027 (quoted in Trench, *On Miracles,* p. 9).

" Und wunderbar erscheint ihm ungewohntes nur
    Der unbewundert sieht das Wunder der Natur." Rückert.

[1] The greatest minds have all been most deeply convinced of this; Bp. Butler builds his entire system upon it. Göthe abounds in such sentences as "We are all walking among mysteries and marvels," "The world is full of enigmas." *Gespräche mit Eckermann,* III. 200, &c. The view of the ancient Greek Fathers was that all the universe was a hymn and a harmony in which to us there might appear to be discordant notes though all made sweet accord in the ears of God. See a truly magnificent burst of eloquence in Clemens Alexandrinus, beginning τοῦτό τοι καὶ τὸ πᾶν ἐκόσμησεν ἐμμελῶς καὶ τῶν στοιχείων τὴν διαφωνίαν εἰς τάξιν ἐνέτεινε συμφωνίας, ἵνα δὴ ὅλος ὁ κόσμος αὐτῷ ἁρμονία γένηται. Clem. Alex. *Protrept.* I. 5.

[2] " Les cieux ne racontent plus la gloire de Dieu, mais celle des Kepler et des Newton." Semerie, *Positivistes et Catholiques,* p. 12 (Paris, 1870). La Place said, "In my heaven I find no God;" and Lalande, "I have peered through the heavens for 60 years and have never seen him yet." See Christlieb, *Moderne Zweifel,* 248.

" Trace Science, then, *with Modesty thy guide;*
    First strip off all her equipage of pride."
                            Pope, *Ess. on Man,* II. 433.

indifference,—almost with ostentatious contempt;—which is the truer, the nobler, the seemlier utterance? There is a little flower not uncommon in our gardens, and found wild in some places, the *geranium striatum*, or "pencilled geranium." It has a small and insignificant blossom, but its pale and tender petals are interveined, as though with some monogram of the Divine artist, with delicate and exquisite reticulations of purpling lines. Pluck it, and the botanist will tell you its name, its species, its genus, the class to which it belongs, its habitat, its history, its variations; but could he produce so much as one fibre of its tissue, or one freak of purple jet upon its leaf? can he tell you the cause of but one vein in the exquisite design upon the corolla of that tiny and tender weed? or look through the microscope at any one of the forms of life which it reveals[1]; at some diatom, fluted and enchased with radiant tracery of more fantastic loveliness than any Moorish arabesque; or at some desmid gleaming like an animated opal with living iridescence, and ask the man of science what he knows[2]?

[1] Ehrenberg found that a cubic inch of tripoli contained 41,000,000 siliceous shells of fossil infusoria. Truly, as Linnæus said, "*Natura præstat in minimis.*" Compare the exquisite lines of Tennyson:
> " See what a lovely shell
> Small and pure as a pearl,
> Lying close to my feet,
> *Frail, but a work divine,*
> Made so fairly well
> With delicate spire and whorl," &c.

[2] "Science also is mute in reply to these questions. But if the materialist is confounded and science is dumb, who else is entitled to answer? To whom has the secret been revealed? *Let us lower*

Not only can he not,—with all the elements for his materials, and all the world for his laboratory,—not only can he not create or evoke the very humblest, meanest, clumsiest form of life,—not one bacterium, not one animalcule, not one film of protaplasm[1],—but he cannot even, with all his vaunted knowledge, discriminate between spontaneous activity and living will[2], nor with all the rich and innumerable and multiplex varieties of life around him, can he so much as flattter himself that he has even approximated to the most distant definition of what life may really be[3].

our heads and acknowledge our ignorance, one and all." Prof. Tyndall, *Address at Norwich*, 1868.

[1] The supporters of spontaneous generation have, as Janet observes, been driven to take refuge in the sphere of the invisible. Up to the present time, at any rate, the delicate and exquisite experiments of M. Pasteur may be regarded as decisive.

[2] The *Æthalium Septicum*, which occurs on decaying vegetable substances, is, in another condition, actively locomotive, and appears to feed on solid matters. "Is this a plant? or is it an animal? is it both? is it neither? Some decide in favour of the last supposition and establish an intermediate kingdom, a sort of biological 'no man's land' for all these questionable forms. But as it is admittedly impossible to draw any distinct boundary line between this 'no man's land' and the vegetable world on the one hand, or the animal on the other, it appears to me that the proceeding merely doubles the difficulty which before was single." Huxley, *Lay Sermons*, p. 14.

[3] The various definitions of life are all of the nature of definitions which define nothing, "mere paraphrases of the thing to be defined, e.g., '*Life is the result of organization,*' Stahl. '*The double interior motion, general and continuous, of composition and decomposition,*' De Blainville. '*The sum of all the functions by which death is resisted,*' Bichat. '*Polarity is the form of its process, and the tendency to progressive individuation the law of its direction,*" Coleridge, *Idea of Life*, &c.

Thus then "*omnia exeunt in mysterium*," and the antecedent probability of miracles can only be settled by the known and indisputable evidence that they have been performed. For, unless the Man of Science be an absolute atheist, or a believer in the eternity of matter, can he deny that God *has* taken direct miraculous part in the construction of the Universe? He may accept the nebular hypothesis, but even then must he not admit that the fluid haze was not automatous, and did not spontaneously evolve its rolling planets and flaming suns? He may accept the Darwinian theory, but even then he must account for the intervention which nucleated the first particle of protoplasm, or quickened the primeval cell with that all-producing principle of development which was to end in the million diversities alike of microscopic and colossal life[1]. If he admit that matter was not eternal, then he must also admit that something material had an immaterial cause. Here then are miracles, and miracles the most stupendous; breakages in the unbroken continuity; mutations in the imagined immutability. And if there have been one such inter-

[1] A. von Humboldt, in one of his letters to Varnhagen von Ense (p. 117), complains of the "scientific levity" with which Strauss finds no difficulty in deriving the organic from the inorganic. Franz Hoffman calls this kind of materialism "a massive conglomerate of intrinsic contradictions....Here change is said to originate from the unchangeable, motion from absolute rest, life from the dead, sense from the senseless, purpose from blindly-acting causes, intelligence from the unintelligent, spirit from the unspiritual" (quoted by Hettinger, *Apolog. des Christenthums*, p. 171). For some very forcible remarks on Materialism, see Mazzini's *Letter on the Œcumenical Council (Fortnightly Review, June,* 1870).

vention, why not—since obviously time is no element in the consideration—why not a myriad? If the chain of apparent causations *began*, why may it not *end*, why may it not be indefinitely modified? If there were an immediate exercise of the divine power to create, why may there not have been to save? If God evoked the agency of laws to produce the *stasis*, why should it be deemed impossible for Him to supervene in remedy of the *apostasis*? Contradiction to His own nature there can be none, for the term nature is confessedly unintelligible if it do not include the idea of its originator[1]. And if He allows the will and the genius of man to modify so largely the action of His elemental forces, and to change so enormously the aspect of His creation, shall He not reserve the same privilege for Himself? It may be said truly that man's will never yet reversed a law of nature; no, but it subjects these laws to modifications, it combines them with the action of other forces, it superinduces on them new conditions. It is the nature of things to gravitate towards the centre of the earth, and yet a balloon of vast weight and containing many persons will rise majestically and rapidly to the clouds, and burst every impediment which would keep it down. To a savage the result might well appear to be miraculous, nor would it be easy to make him understand that the balloon rises in virtue of the very same law which makes

---

[1] See Lange, *Leben Jesu*, II. iii. 9, Mozley, *Bampton Lect.* p. 24. "The existence of a God assumed, the law of the Divine Nature is as much a law of nature as the law which it suspends." This is a complete answer to the objection of Spinoza, *Tract. Theol. Polit.* VI. *De Miraculis.*

the pebble fall. May it not be so with the acts of God? It was pointed out long ago by an English metaphysician that in a miracle the same cause does not produce different effects, but *new* effects are due to wholly *new* causes : no law of nature is violated, no proportion in the cosmic harmony disturbed; but each, preserving its own full effect and influence, combined with a *fresh* influence produces a miraculous result.

You find yourself face to face with one of the great miracles of Christianity ; you try to imagine that scene in which the intensity of one potent voice thrilled into the dim infinitudes of death, and the soul of him who heard it reanimated his lifeless frame, and bound hand and foot in grave-clothes he came forth once more a living man :—or you try to realise how once, on a low Judean hill, in the full blaze of an oriental morn, one who had been crucified, ascended visibly into heaven, and "a cloud received Him out of their sight;" and you dwell on these till you are staggered by their impossibility, and half disbelieve their truth. You recall all that you have observed of the uniformity of nature—you remember the unvarying continuity of its majestic phenomena, and then remembering that man is fallible, and evidence often weak, you are tempted—but before you are led into that conclusion, pause ! Do not be like those whose ears, because they live by the margin of the cataract, are deaf to the roaring of its waves. You are approaching the comtemplation of miracles by a wrong avenue, you are gazing at them under a delusive light. These are not common facts, but signs and powers wrought, not according to man's experience, but according to God's will; they belong not to the same order as the sunrise and the sunset, but to the series of events in which are included the creation of matter and the origin of life. They cannot be excluded by an induction, or rejected by an analysis; they belong not to the physical, but to the spiritual domain. And therefore they must be approached from below upwards, not from above downwards. "*Quousque humi defixa tua mens erit* [1]?" may Theology ask of her sister Science. He whose eyes are for ever on the dust cannot see the stars. If the inorganic crystal does not confute the presumptuous arrogance which can measure its angles but throw no light on the laws of its accretion, then rise from the inorganic to the organic[2]. The path of the lightning which shineth from the east even unto the west you can determine, and you can bind your messages upon the flaming wings wherewith at your bidding it will girdle the habitable globe; even of the wind which bloweth where it listeth you can catalogue the causes and trace the course; but can you set the lark's song to determinate music as it flickers into

---

[1] Cic. *Somn. Scip. ad init.* "Sacrilegii enim vel maximi instar est humi quærere quod in sublimi debeas invenire." Min. Felix, *Octav.* XVII. He who would see Christ transfigured, must, as Origen says, climb the hill; below are crowds, demoniacs, and faithless disciples. Orig. *c. Cels.* VI. 77; cf. Bacon, *De. Augm. Scient.* X. 1: "Animus ad amplitudinem mysteriorum pro modulo suo dilatetur, non mysteria ad angustias animi constringantur."
"Say what the use were finer optics given,
T' inspect a mite, not comprehend the heaven?"
Pope, *Ess. on Man.* I. 196.

[2] Lange, *Leben Jesu*, II. iii. 9.

the blue, or predict the beating of the eagle's wings as it soars upwards amid the storm? You may number every bone and muscle of the ox or the elephant, but can you tell how, as the magic eddy of transformation weaves its unseen agency, the grass and the flower are transmuted indifferently into the juicy pulp or the solid ivory [1]? That a dead man should come back to life you arrogantly declare to be inconceivable,—is it more conceivable how from the void of non-existence a living soul was drawn [2]? You pronounce it impossible that, after the rigour of death and the flaccidity of corruption, the veins should flash once more into healthy life; how is it more possible that, in the womb of her that is with child, should begin the systole and the diastole of the beating heart, and the unapproachable individuality of the living soul? The event is in no respect greater, it is only different. And are all God's actions uniform and homogeneous even in the visible sphere? do you really believe that man is nothing more than thinking matter, or that, as modern materialism expresses it, he *is* only what he *eats*[3]?" Consider *yourself,*—the " abysmal deeps " of your personality—the electrical rapidity of your thoughts—the iron

[1] Coleridge, *Aids to Reflection.*

[2] Quid novi tibi eveniet? Qui non eras, factus es; quum iterum non eris fies." Tert. *Apolog.* XLVIII.; cf. Eccl. xi. 5.

[3] " Was der Mensch *isst*, das *ist* er." Feuerbach, *Gottheit, Freiheit, und Unsterblichkeit.* Thus, as Luthardt observes, *Apologet. Vorträge* (Engl. Tr. p. 130), "Morality ceases to exist, Ethics are converted into a bill of fare." The natural consequence of such a doctrine is that there is no such thing as sin, and therefore no justice in punishment. " A non-sensuous being," says Moleschott, "is nonsense." *Physiol. des Stoffwechsels,* XII.

determination of your purpose—the subtle influences of your intellect—the unutterable mystery of your free will —the unimaginable realms to which you rise in the exaltation of faith, and hope, or even in the phantasies of dreaming sleep; yourself the most stupendous of miracles, will you deny their possibility[1]? If *your* volition counts for so much in the course of events, shall *God's* count for nothing? or will you not rather exclaim with our own great Bacon, "*The soul of man was not produced by heaven or earth, but was breathed immediately from God; so the ways and dealings of God with spirits are not included in nature, that is in the laws of heaven and earth, but are reserved to the law of His secret will and grace*[3]"?

And so, at last—even if, as in the vision of the poet, each step crumble behind us into the darkness[3]—still, "springing from crystal step to crystal step," we are caught up into the heaven of heavens, and see things which it is not possible for man to utter; we spring upon the wings of faith over the boundless gulf, and pass from man to God[4]. And there, in those infinite abysses; there, in that white radiance of an unstained eternity; there, with Him to Whose vision the whole starlit sky is

---

[1] See a fine passage in Mozley, *Bampton Lectures*, p. 90. "Le premier des miracles c'est Dieu. Il y en a un second, c'est l'homme." Guizot, *Méditations sur l'Ess. de la Rel. Chrét.* p. 257.

[2] Bacon, *A Confession of Faith*, quoted by Mozley, *Bampton Lectures*, p. 90.

[3] Cf. *Tennyson, Idylls of the King*, Sir Galahad.

[4] "'Par delà tous ces cieux le Dieu des cieux réside,' a dit Voltaire, et ce Dieu...n'est pas la nature personifiée, c'est le surnaturel en personne." Guizot, *L'Eglise et la Soc. Chrétienne*, p. 14.

but as one white gleam in the intense inane; there,
where time and death are not; where the wings of
thought sink powerless amid the void; where, safe in His
invisible keeping, rest the unnumbered myriads of the
dead; there, what is man? and what is a miracle, that
we should deny the possibility thereof to God? Are we
there in a region in which we can breathe so securely,
walk so confidently, reason so audaciously, impose so
confidently upon the Infinite, the Unseen, the Eternal
Creator, the petty forms of our limited imbecility [1]?
Nay, rather let us abhor ourselves in ashes; let us adore
Him in the dust.

And yet think not, my brethren, that Christianity
fosters a tone of abjectness [2] in the minds of men. Oh!
surely if we had no other God save those great elemental forces which are infinite as compared with man—
which are "stern as fate, absolute as tyranny, merciless
as death—which are too vast to praise, too inexorable

---

[1] "Wunder auf Erden sind Natur in Himmel." J. P. Richter.

[2] Celsus made against Christianity the counter-charge, that it ridiculously over-exalted mankind. Clemens Alex. reproaches Paganism with its contempt for man, and says that Christianity only humbles him that it may afterwards exalt, *Protrep.* x. 114. This is a favourite theme of the Greek Fathers. Orig. *c. Cels.* IV. 25. The charge of fostering abjectness of mind may possibly be more true of Roman Catholicism : "Catholicism, says Dr. Ward, regards Christian virtue as consisting of the will's *abject* prostration before Almighty God : but these Christians [Protestants generally] condemn such an attitude of the mind as degrading and unmanly ; and since they happen to be our fellow-countrymen they further brand it as un-English." *Ess. on Rel. and Lit.* ed. by Archbishop Manning, p. 36 ; and at p. 40 he speaks of the duty of "struggling to live in a constant sense of *abject* dependence upon God."

to propitiate—which have no ear for prayer, no heart for sympathy, no arm to save[1]"—then indeed what could we be but abject? But is it to be abject to know that our being places us far above all these forces in majesty; that the God who wields them all as a very little thing is *our* God, and shall be our guide unto death; that we are His people and the sheep of His pasture; that we may approach Him and ask for His forgiveness; that we may pray to Him and be certain of His love? And how do we know this? only because the only-begotten Son which is in the bosom of the Father, He hath declared Him. And this we know alike by the lessons which He taught, and the deeds He did. And here comes in the true force and meaning of miracles, the immense importance of their evidential purpose[2]. They were no

[1] Holyoake; cf. Tennyson, *In Memoriam:*

"Who trusted God was Love indeed,
And Love creation's final law;
Though Nature, *red in beak and claw*,
With ravine, shriek'd against his creed."

[2] Luthardt, *Ueber die Heilswahrheiten des Christenthums*, p. 202, sqq. collects several similar testimonies: "Die Natur predigt den erdrückendsten Fatalismus, die *unerbittlichste Consequenz*," Röper, *Der Friede in der Schöpfung*, &c. "*Die Natur ist grausam*," Auerbach, *Auf der Höhe*, III. 234. "La Nature ne m'offre rien qui ne soit matière de doute et d'inquiétude," Pascal. See too the wonderful Aphorisms on Nature by Göthe (translated by Professor Huxley, *Nature*, Nov. 4, 1869). "She tosses her creatures out of nothingness, and tells them not whence they came or whither they go......She wraps man in darkness and makes him for ever long for light. She creates him dependent upon the earth, dull and heavy; and yet is always shaking him until he attempts to soar above it." It seems inevitable that the study of nature *alone*, and

mere objectless prodigies, no mere thaumaturgic feats intended to astound the feeble understanding; but they were the Divine proofs of a tender and condescending love [1]. Had they never been performed, we should long ago have been left "having no hope, and without God in the world [2];" long ago, oppressed by the unbroken silence, we might well have believed that there was no living and personal God, or no God for us; and that behind the vail of the blue heavens, as behind the temple-vail through which the rash Roman burst into the Holy of Holies, there were *vacua omnia*. Shut up in the prison-house of imperfect and delusive sense,—denizens of a universe, which being abandoned to dead laws is but "a machine worn by the dust of its own grinding,"—struggling with irresistible forces, the least of which might at any moment annihilate our race,—haunted by ghastly imaginings which spring from the certainties of misfortune, the agonies of suffering, the grinning irony of death,—what, without a knowledge of God, would life have been, or man have been? Surely then

> "Dragons of the prime
> That tare each other in their slime,
> Where mellow music matched with him."

But from all this—which, as all history shows, would to the exclusion of religious truth, should lead to the most despairing pessimism.

[1] "Miracula sunt doctrinæ tesseræ ac sigilla, &c." Gerhard, quoted in Abp. Trench *On the Miracles*, p. 35.

[2] Eph. ii. 12. The denial of miracles has led Strauss and all his school to the denial of Immortality and a personal God. See extracts from Strauss's various works in Christlieb, *Moderne Zweifel am Christ. Glauben*, p. 456.

have been the inevitable result of a Science apart from Revelation—God saved us. To admit us, as it were, into the very bosom of the Infinite, to quench for us the hopeless terror of the unknown, not to render us abject, but, on the contrary, to make us the sons of God, possessors of all that is strong and beautiful in the visible creation, heirs of all that is bright and glorious in the hopes of Immortality and Heaven, God sent His Son. If God made, if God loved, if He would redeem us, was there not here a *dignus vindice nodus?* Yes; His miracles were but the watchwords and seals of saving truth. For our sakes He gave not the Spirit by measure unto Him;

> "The very God,—think, Abib!—dost thou think?
> So the All-Great were the All-Loving too;
> So through the thunder comes a human voice,
> Saying, 'Oh heart I made, a heart beats here.
> Face my hands fashioned, see it in myself;
> Thou hast no strength, nor mayst conceive of mine;
> But love I gave thee, with myself to love,
> And thou must love me who have died for thee[1].'"

[1] Browning, *Men and Women* (*Ep. of Karshish*).

II.

THE ADEQUACY OF THE GOSPEL RECORDS.

"...Which he may read that binds the sheaf,
Or builds the house, or digs the grave,
And those wild eyes that watch the wave
In roarings round the coral reef."
                    Tennyson, *In Memoriam.*

2 PET. I. 16.

For we have not followed cunningly-devised fables when we made known unto you the power and coming of our Lord Jesus Christ, but were eye-witnesses of his majesty.

"NOT on the false track of myths, artificially elaborated "—οὐ γὰρ σεσοφισμένοις μύθοις ἐξακολουθήσαντες [1]. In such words more than 1800 years ago did St Peter [2] anticipate and reject the gnostic theories which began so early to trouble the Church, and which have sprung up in modern times, thick and rank as grass upon the housetops. The expression agrees with the calm declaration of St Paul, that they, the Apostles, were not as the many who trafficked with, who adulterated (in one place οὐ καπηλεύοντες, in another μηδὲ δολοῦντες), *i.e.*, who falsified, mutilated, misrepresented the word of God,—but as of sincerity, but as of God, in the sight of God,

---

[1] τὸ ἐξ errorem notat. Bengel.
[2] I may be allowed incidentally and *en passant* to quote this Epistle as having been written by St Peter, without entering into the controversy about its genuineness.

so spake they in Christ[1]. Such were the deliberate claims of men pre-eminently holy, pre-eminently truthful, pre-eminently soberminded; of men so widely different that the one was but a simple provincial fisherman with no power or inspiration save what he had derived from the Holy Spirit of God, and the other was a man whose boyhood had been passed in the most learned of heathen, and his youth in the most sacred of Jewish cities; and yet both of whom, having given their clear testimony to facts for which both suffered a martyr's death, are now, on no grounds save those of an unphilosophical prepossession, contemptuously waived aside as idle dreamers whose fictions were only, if at all, excusable on the score of idealising mysticism or superstitious credulity.

A second step, then, in our inquiry awaits us, no less needful than the last.

If it be our object, my brethren, in these Lectures, to test as it were the strength of these buttresses on which leans the great edifice of historic Christianity, then the inquiry which occupied us last Sunday was not only important but indispensable. For the Divinity of our Blessed Lord is the central question of modern theology, and it is chiefly denied by those whose abandonment of all belief in the supernatural has been due to the very prepossessions which we endeavoured to remove. Strauss, the coryphæus of modern scepticism, on the one hand avows that his standpoint was the

---

[1] 2 Cor. ii. 17, οὐ καπηλεύοντες τὸν λόγον τοῦ Θεοῦ, cf. iv. 2, μηδὲ δολοῦντες τὸν λόγον τοῦ Θεοῦ.

philosophy of Hegel[1], and on the other starts with the emphatic dogma—a dogma which he assumes as unworthy of further demonstration—that whatever Christ was or did, he can have done nothing which was superhuman or supernatural[2].

If then we have seen that an *a priori* rejection of the miraculous is unphilosophical, and that it is absurd to attempt "the settlement of historic problems by philosophic categories," we arrive at this point—that the credibility of miracles is in each instance simply and solely a question of evidence, and consequently that our belief or rejection of the Christian miracles must mainly depend on the character of the Gospels in which they are recorded. Now into the question of the genuine-

[1] The relation of Strauss to the philosophy of Hegel was this: Hegel had left undefined the relation of the *historical* Jesus to the idea of God-in-man; his orthodox followers had endeavoured to fill up this blank by showing that the Idea, being necessary, must have found its fulfilment in a real person, namely in Jesus of Nazareth. Strauss, by the application of historical criticism, showed how essential were the differences between *dogma* and *speculation*, between the *presentation* and the *notion*. See Schwarz, *Gesch. der Neuesten Theologie*, p. 21. "Strauss erklärt die Geschichte Jesu für falsch; Hegel erklärt sie für irrelevant, für völlig gleichgültig." Hafermann, *Athen oder Bethlehem?* p. 103.

[2] "Wir wissen gewiss was Jesus nicht war und nicht gethan hat; nämlich, nichts Uebermenschliches und Uebernatürliches." "In the person and acts of Jesus no supernaturalism shall be suffered to remain; *nothing which shall press upon the souls of men with the leaden weigh of arbitrary, inscrutable authority* [how much does that sentence reveal!]...for we can plainly perceive this—that no single gospel, nor all the gospels together, can claim that degree of historical reliability *which would be required in order to make or debase our reason to the point of believing miracles.*" Strauss, *New Life of Jesus*, XII. (Engl. Tr.)

ness and authenticity of the Gospels we need not enter, because for our present purpose it has been sufficiently admitted by the most strenuous opponents of the truths which they reveal [1]. The schemes indeed which have been proposed by rival critics with so much arrogant confidence and mutual contempt, have succeeded to each other in such bewildering multitudes, like waves rushing over waves, that we know not whether most to be astonished at their rapidity or to despise their evanescence [2]. But that the three earliest Gospels at any rate, in some form or other, existed before the siege of Jerusalem, and that they had before the middle of the second century acquired a sacred authority, may be regarded

[1] "The review of evidence with regard to the first three gospels gives this result, that soon after the beginning of the second century certain traces are found of their existence, not indeed in their present form, but still of the presence of a considerable portion of their contents, and with every indication that the source of these contents is derived from the country which was the theatre of the events in question." Strauss, *New Life of Jesus*, ed. I. p. 100. "Qu'il me suffise de dire que plus j'ai réfléchi, plus j'ai été amené à croire que les quatre textes reconnus pour canoniques nous conduisent *très près de l'âge du Christ*, sinon par leur rédaction dernière du moins par les documents qui les composent." Renan, *Et. d'Hist. Rel.* p. 172.

[2] "New hypotheses about the three first gospels...follow each other so rapidly, and are asserted and attacked with so much eagerness, that we almost forget that there is anything else to be considered, and the controversy threatens to be so endless," &c. Strauss, *New Life of Jesus*, Pref. XI. (Engl. Tr.). The main discordance shows itself in the views respecting the Gospel of St John which many regard as the most competent of the four testimonies and others reject as late Alexandrian forgeries. Panætius, who declares that the Phædo was spurious, was held to have been sufficiently answered by the line, Εἴ με Πλάτων οὐ γράψε δύω ἐγένοντο Πλάτωνε.

as a conclusion which has been wrung from the inevitable candour of reluctant adversaries; and even were it otherwise, the genuineness of four at least of St Paul's greatest epistles is undisputed and indisputable, and is not only admitted by Baur himself, but is made the basis for his reconstruction of historical Christianity. We may start therefore with the unchallenged certainty that respecting the Person and the Resurrection of our Lord we possess the contemporary evidence of men who desired to know the truth, who had ample opportunities for ascertaining it, who were ready to die in confirmation of it, who were intellectually incapable of having imagined, morally incapable of having invented it. The world has never refused its assent to any other facts supported by evidence so cogent as are those of the Gospel History; it has given unhesitating assent to many a strange fact which rests on infinitely less. Rousseau was a professed sceptic, yet even Rousseau, carried beyond himself, emphatically declared that the Gospel has characters of truthfulness so striking, so perfectly inimitable that its inventor would have been more astonishing than its hero[1]. Niebuhr was the founder of the acutest and most independent school of historical criticism; yet Niebuhr said, "the man who does not hold Christ's earthly life, with all its miracles, to be as pro-

---

[1] Rousseau, *Emile*, Liv. 4. "Jamais les auteurs juifs n'eussent trouvé ni ce ton ni cette morale; et l'évangile a des caractères de vérité si frappants, si parfaitement inimitables, que l'inventeur en serait plus étonnant que les héros" (*Œuvres Comp.* l. 193, vol. XXXVI. p. 39).

perly and really historical as any event in the sphere of history, I do not consider to be a Protestant Christian [1]."

To the blank atheism and credulous incredulity of those recent controversialists who deny to religion all objective truth, and are not ashamed to accuse the Evangelists of deliberate and conscious fraud, we need not reply. The dignity of controversy is lost if she condescend to enter the arena with the coarse gladiators of an offensive infidelity. Their mere existence serves but to illustrate the dangerous tendency of a scepticism which, beginning by the rejection of Christ, rapidly developed into the denial of a God, and upon the ruins of religion built a system which, while it promised liberty and illumination, ended by preaching the Apotheosis of selfishness and the gospel of Eternal Death. Nor again need we trouble ourselves with any of the exploded attacks upon Christianity, from Celsus and Porphyry, down to Woolston and Voltaire [2]. It were lost labour to slay the slain. Only as we advance to the battle-

---

[1] *Leben Niebuhrs*, II. 344. In another passage (*Lebensnachrichten*, I. p. 470) he points out the totally different spirit to be found in the gospel miracles and in the legends and pseudo-miracles of other religions.

[2] How many could say who was the author or what the date of the *Épître à Uranie* (Voltaire's first assault on Christianity, 1728). His ridicule which was once thought so dangerous, and his merriment over the Bible has been compared to a schoolboy "exciting the cheap laughter of his associates by painting a moustache on some fine antique." Hagenbach, *Germ. Rational.* p. 47 (Engl. Tr.). "Pour s'égayer avec Voltaire du dessein d'Ezechiel ou de Génèse, il faut réunir deux choses qui rendent cette gaîté assez triste, *la plus profonde ignorance, et la frivolité la plus déplorable.*" Benj. Constant, *De la Religion*, II. p. 210.

ments and bulwarks of the yet untaken Sion, let us mark how the hills that girdle them are scattered with the ruined enginery of assaults unblessed by God ; and when we have in imagination entered the Holy City and taken our stand upon her shining walls, we may address the mighty leaders of scepticism, and all their intellectual hosts, in the exultant imagery of the Prophet—"The Virgin, the daughter of Sion, hath despised thee, and laughed thee to scorn; the daughter of Jerusalem hath shaken her head at thee. Whom hast thou reproached and blasphemed? and against whom hast thou exalted thy voice and lifted up thine eyes on high? Even against the Holy One of Israel!"

There are but four systems then of rationalism, which in their general principles can be regarded as still retaining, if indeed they do still retain, an independent vitality; viz. the rationalism of Paulus, the naturalism of Schleiermacher, the development-system of Baur, and the mythicism of Strauss. I say, 'if they still retain,' for Paulus can scarcely be said to have ever had a following; the influence of Schleiermacher, powerful as it was, was less the influence of a system than of an intense and glowing mind ; Strauss reckons a greater number of adherents in other countries than in his own; and at Tübingen, the university of Baur, there is a Tübingen school no more [1]. But though the systems have perished, the general effects remain. And therefore, however painful it may be for the hearts of

[1] See Ewald, *Gesch. Christus, Vorrede,* XXVII. (3rd ed.); Christlieb, *Moderne Zweifel,* 626.

those who believe and adore, and who feel a necessary shock to their moral sense when they see their Lord and Saviour arraigned, as it were, before the tribunal of human criticism, yet the constant re-examination and rejection of the faith once delivered to the saints, has rendered it an imperative duty to look these reasonings in the face. A duty, alas, even before an audience like this. Better indeed it would have seemed, above all on this day, when

"Lo, the clouds begin to shine
About the coming of the Lord,"

to endeavour, by God's grace, rather to move the heart than to convince the intellect; better to have set forth with such clearness as might have been vouchsafed some of those lessons, weighty with the solemn issues of death, judgment and eternity, which have been taught by the sweet and bitter experience of advancing life; better to have shown that though no voice from heaven may ever have uttered them in pulses of articulated air, yet in the laws of nature, in the revelation of conscience, in the history of nations, in the fate of individuals—no less clearly than in the lessons of Scripture, no less clearly than though He had written them in fire amid the stars of heaven— "*God spake these words, and said.*" But all this is not our duty now; and when, on the other hand, I remember how in a short year or two many of those who hear me will be scattered for hallowed ministrations among the towns and villages of England; when I recall the inevitable certainty with which ere long these doubts will be arrayed before their minds with all the splendour of eloquence and all the majesty of erudition; when I think that there is no worse symptom of national dissolution than when the faith of her priests has been eaten away by the long corrosion of unacknowledged doubt; then it seems to me that a few moments will not be wasted if the voice of even the feeblest may be heard declaring, why, having earnestly considered what has been urged by those who have argued that Christ rose not, and that His dust yet lies in the Syrian town, he still sees in Him " the brightness of the Father's glory and the express image of His Person, upholding all things by the word of His power [1]."

I. Paulus may be regarded as the founder of rationalism, though he did but extend to the New Testament the Euhemerising principles which Eichhorn had applied to the Old. Accepting as historical the records of Christ's life, he yet eliminated the supernatural by distinguishing between an objective and a subjective element, between fact and judgment, between the events which really happened and the miraculous tinge which they received from the admiration of the Evangelists. They were, he said, credulous exaggerations of fortunate coincidences, or superstitious views of a certain medicinal success[2]. The star of the shepherds was a me-

[1] Heb. I. 3.
[2] St Paul's claim to miraculous powers (2 Cor. xii. 12; Rom. xv. 19; Gal. iii. 5; Heb. ii. 4) is alone sufficient to overthrow this theory. See Christlieb, *Moderne Zweifel*, p. 464. Renan criticises Paulus with his usual delicate tact and discrimination in *Et. d'Hist. Rel.* 140—146: "Jamais," he says, "ne s'était mieux réalisée l'ingenieuse allégorie des filles de Minée changées en chauves-souris pour

teoric exhalation, or a lamp upon the road; the miracle
of Cana was a bridal jest; Christ walked not upon the
sea but along its marge; the Transfiguration was but the
spectral refraction of a mountain haze; the angels in the
tomb were two white-robed Essenes, or the gleam of the
cerements laid aside by one who had been but in a
swoon. The absurdity of the system was its sufficient
refutation. The floating principles of rationalistic interpretation were rendered ludicrous by being gathered into
a focus. It was easier to believe in miracle itself than
in the wholly unnatural combination of ecstasies, light-
ning-flashes, dreams, storms, and mists evoked by the
Rationalists in support of their hypothesis. Paulus indeed may be regarded as the destroyer of rationalism
no less than its founder; it simply dissolved under the
scornful analysis to which Strauss subjected it[1], and the
inseparability of the supernatural from the records of
Christ's life was conclusively demonstrated by the arguments of those who rejected their authority.

II. The refutation extends far beyond the naïve
rationalism of Paulus; it is equally conclusive against the
naturalism of Schleiermacher, and of that very eminent
school of German theologians, who, without absolutely

avoir critiqué comme choses sérieuses les doctrines vulgaires,"
p. 174.

[1] "Here in trying to grasp the pure fact under his guidance we
tumble right into the mire; and assuredly dross, not gold, is the
issue to which his interpretation generally leads......*If the gospels
are really and truly historical, it is impossible to exclude miracles from
the life of Jesus;* if, on the other hand, miracles are incompatible
with history, then the gospels are not really historical records."
Strauss, *New Life of Jesus*, p. 19 (Engl. Tr.).

denying the possibility of miracles, reduce those of our Lord in great measure to the ascendency of a sweet and powerful individuality over the nervous and the insane. Against the noble character and venerable name of Schleiermacher[1] I would not say a word; but it is abundartly clear that he could only mark a transitional epoch. The eclectic Christologies which date from him may be, and often are, morally noble and imaginatively beautiful; but they can have neither a scientific nor a theological value. They are like pieces of subtle jewelry exquisitely specious, and for their ingenuity quite admirable; but which, after admiring their workmanship, we cast aside when we are convinced of the spuriousness of the separate stones out of which they have been wrought. Half views about miracles are no longer possible. They must either be frankly accepted or honestly rejected. Now even if it were admitted that some miracles of healing were conceivably of this character, what would be gained as against the hypothesis of the supernatural? Should we have advanced a single step towards account-

[1] It is almost impossible to exaggerate the profound influence exercised by Schleiermacher and his mediation-system (*Vermittelungs-Theologie*) throughout the entire domain of German Theology. Schwarz mentions Twesten, Nitzsch, J. Müller, Neander, Ullmann, Umbreit, Lücke, Olshausen, Hagenbach; and in another direction De Wette, Baumgarten-Crusius, Hase, Bleek, Thilo, Gieseler, Credner, Schweizer; and again in other directions, Hofmann and others—all more or less impregnated with his methods and formulae. In fact, the impulse which he gave to Theology extended in one extreme to Kliefoth and ecclesiasticism, in the other to Baur and Strauss with their destructive criticism. *Gesch. d. Neuest. Theolog.* p. 27.

ing for the miracles of power[1], for the feeding (for instance) of the multitudes, or the changing of the water into wine? And what should we then say of the mighty central miracle of the Resurrection from the dead? The hazy, wavering manner in which this is slurred over by theologians who still claim the name of Christian—their disappearance from the discussion in a cloud of vague generalities and nebulous mysticism—the impression which they leave of being unable to deny, yet unwilling to admit, is deeply painful and hardly straightforward; but surely the question before us is one in which it is impossible

> "Idly to finger some old Gordian knot,
> Unskilled to sunder yet too weak to cleave,
> And with much toil attain to *half-believe*[2]."

For he who has persuaded himself to reject the Resurrection of Christ, need have no hesitation in rejecting all His other miracles; and if, on the other hand, we heartily believe that Christ's soul was not left in hell, neither did His flesh see corruption, then the reverent acceptance of all His other miracles becomes a simple and an easy faith.

III. So that in fact all these half-rationalistic schools being crushed by the logical consistency of a bolder scepticism, we must either with Baur degrade the Gospels into ideal fictions, or with Strauss, sublimate them into credulous myths.

---

[1] See some forcible remarks in Prof. Westcott's *Characteristics of the Gospel Miracles* pp. 15—20

[2] Clough's Poems, p. 68.

The scheme of Ferdinand Christian von Baur[1], the Porphyry of modern criticism, treated the Gospels as representing not the reality of events, but the objectising of imaginations and tendencies. He aimed at proving that the history of Christ's life was the necessary result of Greek speculation, Jewish monotheism, and Roman Empire. Surely there are some very simple principles which at once throw discredit on such a scheme in spite of his immense industry and wealth of erudition. In the first place, it assumes the strange doctrine that great national tendencies find their satisfaction not in events corresponding to them, but in the mere elaboration of self-conscious fictions: and next, it conspicuously fails in the attempt to prove that the fiction had any resemblance to known and definite expectations. In the first place, Christianity, so far from being a system of doctrine, is so purposely unsystematic, that men have deduced from it the most widely different truths; in the next place, it barely alludes, and that not favourably,

---

[1] The most important critical inquiries of Baur were subsequent to the first publication of Strauss's *Leben Jesu* in 1835; but they modified the views of Strauss in several important particulars, and on the whole unfavourably. Strauss himself rightly points out how entirely untenable is Baur's notion that his system was the less destructive of the two. Schwarz thus sums up Baur's views: "Das Christenthum ist nicht ein von vornherein fertiges, ein vollkommenes und himmlisches Product; es ist vielmehr, ein sich *allmählig entwickelndes*. Und der Boden, aus welchem es sich entwickelte, war das Judenthum." *Gesch. d. Neuest. Theolog.* p. 156. Comte's view was somewhat similar. See a paper by Prof. Westcott on "Comte and Christianity," in the *Contemp. Rev.* VII. 404 sqq., which, like all that comes from his pen, is of permanent value.

either to Greek philosophy or to Roman Empire,— of all that is noble in which it was the heir, but not the issue [1] But further than this it was in flagrant disaccord with the ideal of the society in the bosom of which it rose. So far from satisfying the tendencies of the age or the nations which watched it dawn, it united them in a conspiracy of common detestation [2]. As a Teacher, the bearing of Christ was in violent contrast with that of the stately priests and scrupulous Pharisees who possessed the unbounded confidence of the people [3], but on whose

[1] With all its historic research and criticism, Baur's theory is utterly unsubstantial; it is not too much to say that it breaks down at every point. As to the Greeks, the humility and childlikeness demanded by Christianity cut at the very root of their philosophic pride; its perfect openness rebuked their esoterism; its obscure and barbarous origin repelled their patriotic feelings; its stern purity branded even a Zeno or a Diogenes with shame. In fact a Rabbi and a Sophist were the interlocutors in the deadly polemic of Celsus. To them the preaching of the cross was foolishness, and a stumbling-block; it was neither a sign nor wisdom. See 1 Cor. i. 18—23: Is. viii. 14; Acts xvii. 18. See Arnob. *adv. Gent.* I. 40, "Sed patibulo affixus interiit!" cf. 36, "*crucis supplicio interemptum et Deum fuisse contenditis!*"

[2] See Æsch. *Prom.* V; Plato, *Alcib.* II. 150; *Rep.* pp. 271—275; Phædo, p. 85; Virg. *Ecl.* IV. (Cf. Aug. *de Civ. Dei*, X. 27.) *Æn.* VI. 27; Suet. *Vesp.* 4, 5; Dio, *Vesp.* 64; Tac. *H.* V. 13, I. 10; Jos. *de B. Jud.* V. 3.

[3] Jos. *Antt.* XIII. 10. 6. νόμιμα πολλά τινα παρέδοσαν τῷ δήμῳ, id. 15. 5, δύνασθαι δὲ πολὺ παρὰ τοῖς Ἰουδαίοις ἔφασκε βλάψαι τε μισοῦντας καὶ φίλους διακειμένους ὠφελῆσαι, κ.τ.λ. A modern Rabbi (Geiger, *Ueber das Judenthum und d. Gesch.* 1865) has made the astounding remark that Jesus was a Pharisee of the School of Hillel! On this subject see Salvador, *Jésus Christ et sa Doctrine*, passim. For the bearing, &c. of Rabbis, see Sepp, *Leben Christi*, II. p. 47.

guilty heads He kindled the scathing flame of His tenfold malediction. As a Prophet, He claimed the credentials of miracles, which, in others of the very greatest prophets, had been considered superfluous, and He refused the very miracles which were demanded at His hands[1]. As a Messiah, He reversed and violated the most cherished expectations of His land and age[2]. In the *Memorabilia* of Xenophon, in the *Eclogues* of Virgil we may see the type of Deliverer for whom the Gentiles yearned,—a Philosopher who should resolve all questions, a princely Infant before whom the rocks should flow with honey, and the briars bloom with rose. In Judas the Gaulonite,—a man of traditional belief, of dazzling eloquence, of burning patriotism, of undaunted courage,— in Barkokebas, an impetuous boaster, a lying sorcerer,

[1] That He did so was another objection of Celsus, Orig. *c. Cels.* 1. 68; see Matt. xvi. 1; Luke xvii. 20, 21.

[2] Even His most chosen disciples rejected with horror the first announcement of His approaching sufferings, Matt. xvi. 22. Bruno Bauer attempts to prove that there was no Messianic conception; Gfrörer that there were *four* types of Messiah. Both exaggerations at least show how little ground there is for the supposition that the history of our Lord was a romance founded on *a priori* beliefs. The subject has been examined with profound learning by Schöttgen, *Horæ Hebr. et Talmudicæ*, 1733; Hilgenfeld, *Messias Judæorum;* Nork, *Rabbinische Quellen*, 1839. Gfrörer, *Das Jahrhundert des Heils*, 1838. An analysis of the chief certain conclusions may be found in Prof. Westcott's *Introd. to the Study of the Gospels*, pp. 86—151. Dorner, after examining the Talmudic notions about Adam Kadmon, Memra (=λόγος), Shechinah, Metatron, &c. ends . "*Zu der Idee einer Incarnation der wirklich Göttlichen aber haben es alle diese Theologumene insgesammt nie gebracht.*" *Entwickelungsgesch. von der Person Christi*, 1. p. 60 (1845). That the Jews expected the Messiah to be *a man* is clear from Justin *c. Tryph.* c. 48.

and an iron-handed chief, we may see the type of the Messiah for whom the Jews had looked[1]. They expected "a more victorious Joshua, a more magnificent Herod, a wider-ruling Cæsar, a wiser Moses, a holier Abraham[2]," not the Nazarene, the carpenter, the crucified; not one in whom the glorious passion of their poet-prophets became a perfect simplicity, and the fire which had burnt before them a lambent flame. The path that "nobly desired to descend,"—the greatness, not of self-assertion, but of self-sacrifice[3],—the light which would not blaze with noonday splendour, but shone quietly in the uncomprehending darkness,—the glory which was greater than the glory of Solomon, though it chose not the purple of sovereignty, but the form of a servant,—what did they know of these? The idea of one who was crowned indeed, but only with a crown of thorns,—uplifted, but only on the throne of the

---

[1] The name Barkokab (בר כוכב) means "son of a star." In the Jewish Sibylline oracles (*circ.* A.D. 140) the Messiah descends from the sun. Compare the fine lines of Heber:

"He comes, but not in regal splendour drest,
The haughty diadem, the Tyrian vest;
Not armed in flame, all glorious from afar,
Of hosts the Captain, and the Lord of War," &c.

One of the Talmudic legends was that he should force the sea to empty at his feet on the shore at Joppa all its pearls and all its hidden treasures; which, with all the wealth of the world since the days of Pharaoh, should be divided among the Jews. Sepp. *Leben Jesu*, § 3, ch. XXV.

[2] Milman, *History of the Jews*, I. p. 80.

[3] μέγας ἐνώπιον τοῦ Κυρίου, Luke i. 15, 32. δόξαν παρὰ ἀνθρώπων οὐ λαμβάνω, John v. 41, vi. 15.

accursed tree[1],—exalted, but only by a sinless innocence—the idea of One who blessed the world with arms outstretched upon the Cross—was created solely by the living fact; and He in whom it was realised, so far from being formed by popular conceptions or secular tendencies, won for Himself during His lifetime only a mere handful of obscure and timid followers, and perished under the banded obloquies of the nations and of His age.

IV. The views of Strauss, in approaching whom we are attacking the very citadel of modern scepticism[2],

[1] It only needs to consult Tertullian's *Ad Judæos*, or Justin Martyr's *Dialogue with Trypho* (see espec. p. 249), to see that Christ's humiliation was to the Jew a most decisive disproof of His Messiahship; the ἐσταυρώθη γάρ was the indignant and horrified clinching of all controversy. See some very interesting notes and quotations in Bp. Pearson *On the Creed*, Art. II. and IV. pp. 124, 261 (ed. 21); yet, after all the learning which has been expended on the subject, it is clear from John vii. 2; Acts xvi. 22; Luke xxiv. 21; Acts xvii. 3, xxvi. 23, viii. 32, that the idea of a suffering Messiah resulted from the teaching of Christ himself, and was not believed till He had risen. In Enoch vii. 29, it is indeed declared that the Christ should die, but only after a splendid reign of 400 years. The idea of a second suffering Messiah, the Son not of David, but of Joseph or of Ephraim (Buxtorf, *Synag. Jud.* p. 717), is only found in later Jewish writings which had been subjected to unconscious Christian influences, but not earlier than the Babylonian Gemara, A.D. 498. As for the *Sepher ha Zohar*, it is not earlier than the 13th century, nor is it certain that its author was not a Christian.

[2] It has been the fashion in Germany to call Strauss's book *ein epochemachendes Werk*, but Schwarz truly observes that it marked "nicht sowohl eine *Epoche* als eine Krise, nicht sowohl einen *Anfangs*- als einen Schlusspunkt." *Gesch. Neuest Theolog.* p. 3. Even Strauss had received his impulse from Schleiermacher, in order to hear whose lectures he went in 1831 from Tübingen to Berlin.

F. H. L 5

were somewhat different. He regarded the miracles not with Paulus, as legends founded on fact,—nor with Schleiermacher as the natural effects of an unusual ascendency,—nor with Baur as fictions developed out of a tendency,—but as myths generated by the idea ; as the crown of supernatural fancies with which, under the influence of Messianic conceptions and religious enthusiasm, the early disciples encircled the brow of their beloved Lord[1]. If He were represented as the Son of a Virgin, it was from the misconception of a passage of Isaiah ; if as feeding the multitudes, it was because Moses had fed the Israelites with manna in the wilderness ; if as missed by His parents in the Temple, it was—will it be believed?—because the Emperor Augustus as a child, having been searched for, high and low, had been discovered reposing at the eastern summit of the house[2].

[1] See Strauss, *Leben Jesu*, Introd. § xv. (Ed. 4) and *passim*. In the Introd. to the *New Life of Jesus* (Eng. Tr. I. 142) he defines myths as 'investitures, resembling history, of original Christian ideas, fashioned in the legend which unconsciously invented them.' Baur, in his *Krit. Untersuch. über die canonischen Evangel.* p. 121, said that the 'mythical theory has been already rejected by every man of education up to the present day.' Strauss, who always speaks of him in terms of the deepest respect, without accepting the idea of *Tendency* which Baur strove to substitute for that of *myth*, yet "mainly in consequence of Baur's hints, allowed more room than before to the *hypothesis of conscious and intentional fiction.*" *New Life*, I. p. 213. And in the Latin Pref. to the Eng. ed. of his first work, he says that Baur first convinced him that the author of the 4th Gospel "*haud raro meras fabulas scientem confinxisse.*"
[2] Strauss, *New Life of Jesus* (Eng. Tr.), II. p. 95. Sueton. *Octav.* 94. The analogies forced into parallelism with gospel incidents are very far fetched ; *e.g.*, the song of the angels is com-

And to these stories Strauss gave the unfortunate name of myths. We know what myths are; they are attempts to explain the forgotten accidents of language, or to allegorise the great phenomena of nature; they belong for the most part to an early and uncritical age, and deal with the cloudy, the mysterious, the vast. In their origin, in their dissemination, in their characteristics, they offer no analogy to the Gospel records. If other theories are true, the Apostles must have been either untruthful or credulous; if this theory be true, they must have been *both:* in the one case, how can we account for their lofty morality? how, in the other, for their unequalled wisdom? They have long been dead, and nations have for ages bent with reverence over their hallowed cenotaphs, but we can imagine with what high authority and burning indignant eloquence they would have shrivelled into nothing these insulting theories to which we listen with such a tame and impartial courtesy. Yes, as they heard them, since they lived not in an age in which generous passion was branded as deficient self-control,—nor yet in their times had the volcanic fires of a strong enthusiasm been stifled under the chill white ashes of a fastidious cynicism,—must we not believe that St John would have been once more the Son of Thunder, and St Paul would have burst into words which are "half battles," and the brow of St Peter would have been clothed with that stern majesty which "strook Simon Magus with a curse;" and if I may have leave to adopt the mighty words of

pared to the voice heard at the birth of Osiris. Plut. *De Isid. et Osir.* XIII.

the poet to whom this University looks with reverence as her loftiest son—'the invincible warrior Zeal, whose substance is ethereal, armed in complete diamond, would have ascended his fiery chariot, and, shaking loosely the slack reins, have driven over the heads of these insulting theories, bruising their stiff necks under his flaming wheels[1].'

But supposing with Strauss that the Gospels are myths, supposing with Baur that they are the results of tendency, who, we ask, were their inventors? Not Jewish Christians certainly of the so-called Petrine faction; for then, even if the myths of their development had not been characterised by all the exclusiveness and fanaticism of the *Book of Jubilees*, yet on Baur's own showing

[1] Milton, *Apology for Smectymnuus;* but I must apologize for altering a few words of that splendid outburst. With the words of my text may be compared the strong language of St Paul in Tit. i. 16; 1 Tim. iv. 7; 2 Tim. iv. 4. The βέβηλοι καὶ γραώδεις μῦθοι might have been still more indignantly described had they been so insultingly delusory as those to which Baur and Strauss would reduce the gospel narratives. The feeblest intellect must see the strangeness of supposing "that the holiest of men was a deceiver, his disciples either deluded or liars, and that deceivers should have preached a holy religion of which self-denial is the chief duty," Niebuhr, *Lebensnachr.* I. 470. "The idea of men writing mythic histories between the time of Livy and Tacitus, and *St Paul mistaking such for realities!*" Arnold, *Life*, II. 58. "Ce Christ *a priori*, on le divine bien, n'est pas encore le Christ historique...La *Vie de Jésus* (of Strauss) n'est au fond que la philosophie du chef de l'école allemande contemporaine, appliquée aux recits évangéliques." Renan, *Et d'Hist. Rel.* pp. 157, 158. "Ist es je in der Welt erhört worden, dass eine ganze Gemeinschaft ein Lebensbild mit einer Fülle einzelner Züge zusammengedichtet hätte?" Ullmann, *Die Sündlosigk. Jesu*, p. 60.

they would have had a deeply Ebionitic tinge ; nor yet Gentile proselytes of the imaginary Pauline faction[1], for they would never have represented Christ as sent mainly and primarily, and in His own personal mission all but exclusively, to the lost sheep of the House of Israel. These theories revolve indeed in a vicious circle, they make the Church account for the religion, and the religion for the Church[2]; and as though we should invoke the world to account for the existence of God, they explain the miracles and character of the Redeemer by the society which He founded. Even in the Apocalypse,

---

[1] If Baur's theory of the deep antagonism and hatred between the Pauline and Petrine schools were true, it would be indeed amazing that one Ideal so pure, so homogeneous, and so perfect should have emanated from their conflicting beliefs. But although undoubtedly the Clementines show that the doctrines of St Paul did cause him to be regarded as ὁ ἐχθρὸς ἄνθρωπος by some Elcesaites, yet the attempts to identify him with the Balaam of the Apocalypse, &c., are simply a large inverted pyramid of inferences resting on an excessively small apex, and can only be accepted by those who regard the Acts of the Apostles and much of the Epistles as deliberately untrustworthy.

[2] "Ce qu'il laisse subsister des Évangiles est insuffisant pour motiver la foi des Apôtres, et l'on a beau admettre chez eux la disposition à se contenter d'un *minimum* de preuve, il faut que ses preuves aient été bien fortes pour vaincre les doutes navrants occasionnés par la mort sur la croix." Renan, *Et. d'Hist. Rel.* p. 168. This has also been pointed out with great force by Ullmann, *Historisch oder Mythisch?* His two strongest points are the belief of St Paul in the Resurrection, and the permanent, undeniable *Fact* of the existence of the Christian Church. Even Bruno Bauer well remarks : "Diese mysteriöse Substantialität der christlichen Gemeinde hat keine Evangelien hervorbringen können, denn sie hat keine Hände zu schreiben, keinen Geschmack zu componiren, keine Urtheilskraft das zusammengehörende zu vereinen." *Kritik. d. Synoptiken*

and in those four Epistles of St Paul, the genuineness of which the Tübingen school admit, Christ appears plainly as God and King[1]. Whence then came a reverence so absorbing, a devotion so unbounded? from His teaching? witness the deep offence taken by His very disciples, and the stones which the Jews took up to stone Him[2]. But had His teaching been ever so deeply admired, why on that account should a Jew *worship* Him, more than his awful Moses, or princely David? or a Greek, more than his subtle Pythagoras and blameless Socrates? or a Roman, more than his stern Cato and many-minded Cicero? And afterwards, when there arose a Marcus Aurelius, the beautiful, noble, warlike emperor of the civilized world, with his exquisite candour and almost faultless morality, and the white flower of his blameless life,—was *he* worshipped[3]? Apollonius of Tyana was not only a favourite teacher but an accredited thaumaturge; yet, as Tertullian says, "*Nemo Apollonium*

[1] Acts vii. 59; Rev. xix. 13, xxii. 20; 1 Cor. i. 2, ii. 8, viii. 6, xv. 47; 2 Cor. iv. 4, cf. Plin. *Epp.* x. 96; Euseb. *Hist.* IX. 14, 21. *Eccl.* v. 28.

[2] Is. viii. 14; Matt. xiii. 57; Acts xiii. 45. Schelling ends a fine passage on this subject with "Nicht die Evangelien sind nothwendig um die Hoheit Christi zu erkennen, sondern umgekehrt, die Hoheit Christi ist nothwendig um diese Erzählungen, um die Evangelien zu begreifen." *Philos. d. Offenbarung*, quoted in Christlieb, *Moderne Zweifel*, 480.

[3] On the contrary, it is clear from the *Meditations* that he was conscious of being personally disliked because of his very virtues. In one melancholy passage he tells us that in spite of his loving, paternal, unselfish care for all about him, yet when he died he was *quite aware that they would say amongst themselves,* "*Thank goodness we have now got rid of this schoolmaster.*"

pro Deo colit." Or was Christ worshipped as a God because of His sufferings? My brethren, if this were all, as far as mere physical anguish is concerned, many of the martyrs suffered more. Yet no Christian worshipped the martyrs, though the Jews and the heathen falsely charged them with doing so[1]. No, the Gospels do not account for Christ; but the reality and the grandeur of Christ are the sole explanation of the possibility of the Gospels. And if, with these facts in view, we read the pages of Strauss, based as they are on an *a priori* assumption, crowded as they are with captious frivolities and arbitrary criticisms, even the scribe who is least instructed in the kingdom of Heaven may face them without dismay, and may lay them down, not indeed without sadness, yet with a strong conviction that God's own hand smites with unconscious paralysis the strength of those whose labour and genius—like desecrated incense upon unhallowed altars—is expended in the cause of unbelief[2].

[1] "We *adore* Christ as the Son of God," wrote the Christians of Smyrna to the Christians of Pontus; "the martyrs, as followers and disciples of our Lord, we *love.*" Euseb. *Hist. Eccl.* IV. 15, quoted by Cave, *Prim. Christianity*, I. 5, cf. Aug. *de Civ. Dei*, viii. 27: "We set apart no temples, nor priests, nor divine services, nor sacrifices to martyrs, *because they are not God.*"

[2] Lacordaire, after describing in his powerful and impassioned style, the effect of Strauss's *Life of Jesus* on his mind (une sorte de frayeur involontaire, causée par l'abundance de l'érudition, &c.), adds, "Eh bien! à part trois ou quatre passages il ne m'a jamais fallu plus de dix minutes pour dissiper la charme d'une vaine science, et sourire au dedans de moi de l'impuissance à laquelle Dieu a condamné l'erreur." *Conférences*, 1846, p. 155.

II. But leaving these more special considerations, it seems to me that there are three broad grounds on which we may safely meet the assaults of Rationalism and Mythicism in any one of the forms which they assume.

i. The first of these is the nature and character of the miracles themselves. An assertion of unlimited miraculous power is so difficult to substantiate that, apart from Christianity, I scarcely know a single instance in which it has been put forward. Prophets of the most splendid reputation did not claim them; St John the Baptist, intensely and powerfully as he swayed the inmost hearts of his nation, was never accredited with them. Founders of great religions—Confucius, Sakya Mouni[1], Zoroaster, Mahomet[2]—even in obscure ages, even amid barbarous surroundings,—made no pretence to them. If, in a few instances, Christian saints have professed to be endowed with them, it has been only in virtue of Christ's power, nor even in *their* legends do they occur in contemporaneous evidence, or in any but instances of a dubious kind[3]. Yet Christ—surrounded

---

[1] See *The Modern Bhuddist* (by a Siamese Minister) translated by Mr Alabaster, p. 217.

[2] Mahomet distinctly disclaimed miracles, and appealed to the *Koran* in lieu of them, so that the paragraphs of the *Koran* are called *aiât*=sign or miracle. The miracles attributed to him in later legends, *e.g.*, that the moon after seven times going round the Kaaba, saluted him, entered his right sleeve, and, slipping out at the left, split into two halves, which reunited after having retired to the extreme east and west, were truly signs from heaven! see Tholuck, *Vermischte Schriften*, I. p. 27.

[3] The arguments in favour of the genuineness of the ecclesiastical and mediæval miracles may be found sketched by the hand of a

as He was by the "immense publicity" of furious Jews, and haughty Romans, and sneering Greeks—not only claimed them, but His claim was undisputed by His deadliest enemies. Neither the Pharisees, nor the multitudes, nor Caiaphas, nor Herod, nor Celsus, nor Porphyry, nor Hierocles, nor Julian dreamt of denying that He *had* wrought deeds apparently supernatural; and it is an insult to the understanding to compare the evidence on which they rest, either with the vulgar travesty of a miracle alleged to have been wrought by a coarse soldier before the rabble of Alexandria[1], or with the posthumous plagiarisms in the heavy romance of the sophist Philostratus. And yet observe that the Gospel miracles are no mere senseless wonders, no soarings on the wondrous Borak, as in the legend of Mahomet, no sitting on fiery cushions in the air as in the *Lalitavistara*, but calm and noble, each involving a deed of mercy, each conveying a lesson of truth[2]. Subservient to the

master in Dr Newman's two celebrated Essays which have just been reprinted. Most of them lying in the ambiguous region of ill-understood pathological facts may safely be accepted when the evidence in their favour is at all reasonable. The supposed thaumaturgic power of St Francis Xavier received no countenance from any claim of his own, and he makes very light indeed of a case in which he was supposed to have resuscitated a dead infant. The contemporary evidence in favour of cures wrought, or said to have been wrought at La Salette, and by the curé d'Ars throws fresh light on the nature of such facts.

[1] Père Cassell, in his little book *Le Roi te Touche*, shows good reasons for believing that this so-called miracle (!) of Vespasian's was itself due to a widespread belief in the miracles of Christ. See Christlieb, *Moderne Zweifel*, p. 473.

[2] See Rowland Williams, *Christianity and Hinduism*, pp. 161

Life of Christ, deriving their greatness from it, treated as insignificant in comparison to that submission of which they were but a single evidence, promised (which is surely most unlike a myth) in yet larger abundance to the immediate followers who believed in Him [1],—miracles such as these are indisputably unique in the world's history; they are the glory and the evidence of Christianity alone. Notice too that they were sternly and invariably refused to a gaping curiosity, or a clamorous unbelief [2]. No mythicist surely could have made what has been called the damaging admission that faith was an essential to their operation; he would have represented them as displayed before competent *savants* [3], so public always as to exclude denial, so powerful always as to enforce assent. But God, while He tenderly helps even the feeblest faith, does not condescend to force the reluctant and external assent of those who would not believe though one rose from the dead. It is not too

—164. "On voit dans l'Évangile que les miracles de Jésus étaient tous utiles, mais ils étaient sans éclat, sans apprêt, sans pompe; ils étaient simples comme ses discours, comme sa vie, comme toute sa conduite." Rousseau, *Lettres de la Montagne*, I. p. 3.

[1] John xiv. 12. "Neque quicquam est ab illo gestum...*quod non omne donaverit faciendum parvulis illis et rusticis* et eorum subjecerit potestati." Arnobius *adv. Gentes*, 1. 50, cf. II. 12.

[2] Orig. *c. Cels.* I. 68.

[3] Mons. Renan insists on this as a necessary criterion of miracles. But how much chance would a miracle have had of recognition before the French Academy, for instance, which rejected the use of lightning-conductors, vaccination, the existence of meteorites, &c. Christlieb, *Moderne Zweifel*, p. 360. It is a strange demand, that if God requires His mighty works to be believed He must submit them to a committee of competent *savants*!

much to say that this reserve of miraculous interference[1],—this dislike of its exercise for any purposes but those of tenderness,—this stern and positive refusal to employ it either in silencing the insults of the inimical, or in gratifying the curiosity of the commonplace,—this frank admission that many of Christ's miracles were calumniated or denied,—are marks of truth and of simplicity such as are found in no similar records of a nascent faith, and such as are so utterly alien from the annals of imposture, that they are alone sufficient, when fully and impartially considered, to crumble the mythical theory of miracles into the dust?

ii. A second general but no less convincing fact is the entire style and character of the Gospels. Written by fishermen and tax-gatherers, who were unlearned and ignorant men, they have yet thrown all other histories into the shade. Only consider, my brethren, what they are to us. In the dim hours of sorrow and bereavement; in the hours when, like a grotto of icicles under the noonday beam, all our vain hopes, all our cherished aspirations are melting into a rain of tears; in the hours of painful lassitude, when we hear

"Time flowing through the middle of the night;"

in the hour when, like an uncertain echo in the lonely corridors of some haunted house, we hear far off the

[1] We may get a true measure of the difference between invention and fact by placing the prodigality of miracles attributed to the infant Saviour in the apocryphal gospels side by side with the "This *beginning of miracles* did Jesus in Cana of Galilee" in the very gospel which is asserted to have been expressly forged in proof of His Godhead!

monotonous footfall of approaching death; what is it that calms, and comforts, and soothes us then? Is it any discovery of science; is it any scheme of philosophy? is it even the sublime vision of Dante, or the lordly eloquence of Milton? is it anything that orator has uttered and poet sung? Nay, when the melody of lyric songs has lost its charm, and the music of memory and her siren daughters has been brought low, we still listen —when we can listen to nothing else—to the Beatitudes which Christ spake to the multitudes as they sat listening among the mountain lilies, or to those last words, more precious than archangel's utterance, which on the same night that He was betrayed He spake to His beloved ones, when the traitor had gone out and it was night And yet the Evangelists are men who frankly describe the tardiness, the imperfection, the vacillations of their own faith; men who in their noble humility do not conceal the strength of their prejudices, the slowness of their enlightenment, the cowardice of their behaviour, the carnality of their belief, and who yet express a sober intensity of conviction, which can find no other explanation than the reality of the events to which they witness. On every page they write is the *simplex veri sigillum*[1]. The paroxysms of excited eulogy, the blush

---

[1] "Jamais la vertu n'a parlé un si doux langage ; jamais la plus profonde sagesse ne s'est exprimé avec tant d'energie et de simplicité... *Voyez les livres des philosophes avec toute leur pompe ; qu'ils sont petits auprès de celui-là !*" Rousseau (*Pensées et Maximes*, p. 36).
"Jamais les auteurs juifs n'eussent trouvé ni ce ton ni cette morale · et l'évangile a des caractères de vérité si frappants, si parfaitement inimitables, *que l'inventeur en serait plus étonnant que les héros.*"

as it were of self-conscious exaggeration, so common in the late thaumaturgic biographies of mediæval saints, find no place in these sweet and noble narratives. Their minute differences establish their independence; their undesigned coincidences attest their truth. And in every case in which it has been possible to vindicate their historical accuracy by confronting their evidence with that of Pagan historians, it has been found to stand the minutest and most searching tests. In the case, for instance, of St Luke, who is invariably treated by rationalists as a mere careless compiler, the minute jealousy of sceptical inquisition combined with the truth-loving labour of Christian research has only tended to establish his historical value and accuracy in the most insignificant details. Sergius, the Proconsul of Cyprus, was believed to have been a Proprætor till St Luke's authority was finally confirmed by the evi-

Id. p. 39. Origen dwells very powerfully on this simplicity of the style of the gospels—those ἰδιωτικοὶ λόγοι—so unlike the fiery and magnificent eloquence of the Prophets, yet possessing a magic infinitely more potent than the words of Plato; a magic learnt not in the schools but by heavenly inspiration. He compares them, not to unwholesome and highly-spiced dainties for the rich, but to good food accessible to the very poorest. *c. Cels.* III. 68, VII. 59, 60.

"Truth in closest words shall fail
When truth embodied in a tale
Shall enter in at lowly doors,

Which they may read who bind the sheaf,
Or build the house or dig the grave,
Or those wild eyes which watch the wave
In roarings round the coral reef."

Tennyson, *In Memoriam.*

dence of coins [1]. Lysanias, tetrarch of Abilene, was ridiculed as a clumsy invention, till even Renan has the candour to admit that his recent examination of the inscription of Zenodorus at Baalbek has led him to believe that the Evangelist was not so gravely wrong [2]. The taxing in the time of Cyrenius, had long been branded as a flagrant and damaging anachronism, till the industry of Zumpt demonstrated that it was an historical datum implied though not recorded by other historians [3]. And yet this is held up to us as the *loosest* of those documents; so calm, so simple, so accurate, so detailed, so harmonious, in which we are asked to see specimens of boundless credulity or wilful fraud. Had they been such, we are happily able to see conclusively the form they would have assumed. The apocryphal Gospels actually were such mythical forgeries. In the meanness, absurdity, and malignity, in the debased style and defective morality, of these worthless Hagadoth, we may see what the Gospels would have resembled had the theories of Baur and Strauss been true. The Gospels are as little like them as the sun in heaven is like the mephitic gleam of the vapour in a mine. We are only

[1] 'Ανθύπατος, Acts xiii. 7   Ackermann's *Numismatic Illustrations to the N. T* p. 41 ; Dio Cass. LIV. 4.

[2] Renan, *Vie de Jésus*, Introd. XIII.

[3] Before the true explanation was known, Wetstein had simply said "Epocha tam celebris non potuit Lucam latere." But Zumpt's remarkable treatise, *Das Geburtsjahr Christi ; Geschichtlich-chronologische Untersuchungen*, Leipzig, Teubner, 1869, leaves no doubt in candid minds that St Luke was right. (What little may *still* be said on the other side by those who are too biased to be convinced may be seen in Strauss, *Die Halben und die Ganzen*, 70—79.)

glad that they should have lingered on in obscure contempt, because they offer so providential a contrast to the true Sibylline utterance, which, in the words of the ablest and perhaps the greatest of Greek philosophers, "with inspired lip speaking things simple, and unperfumed, and unadorned, reacheth over ten thousand years because of God."

iii. But one proof more, and that the most irresistible, remains. It is the transcendent, commanding character, the unique sovereign splendour of the personality of Christ; on every action the stamp of eternity, in every utterance the inspiration of truth. It is strange and touching to see how this character with the winning love of its irresistible tenderness, by the moral sorcery of its infinite self-sacrifice, pervades, astonishes, overwhelms, subdues. Like the armed band who came to seize Him in the garden, His very enemies seem to fall in admiration before His feet, and even the metaphysicians who explain away the divinity of His being, see in Him the best and truest symbol of heavenly wisdom[1], or of ideal perfection[2], or of the union between the human and the divine[3]. And so far has the many-sidedness and richness of His character transcended the thoughtful analysis of the closest observers, that scarcely

[1] Spinoza.   [2] Kant.
[3] Hegel. See Luthardt, *Apolog. Vorträge über die Grundwahrheiten des Christenthums*, X. (Engl. Tr. p. 284). The desire to be considered Christians seems to remain strongly even in those who would utterly overthrow historical Christianity. Strauss says: "Wir finden unsere heutige Weltanschauung *christlicher als die urchristliche selbst.*" *Zwei friedliche Blätter*, 1839.

any man, or section of men, has been able to appreciate more than one of its purely human aspects[1]. The Knights of old saw in Him the mirror of all chivalry;

[1] To Strauss he is a wise Galilæan Rabbi; to Schenkel a sort of party-demagogue, the representative of political and theological progress; to Renan a moral teacher whose dreamy mysticism ended in uncontrolled fanaticism and even conscious deceit. "Ein mysterium," "ein unicum," are phrases used of Him by others, as Hase, Weisse, Schenkel, &c., who do not accept His divinity. "Between Him and whoever else in the world," said Napoleon with profound truth, "*there is no possible term of comparison!*" "Jésus en tout est unique, et rien ne saurait lui être comparé." Renan, *Et. d'Hist. Rel.* p. 175. "Ce Christ évangélique est la plus belle incarnation de Dieu dans la plus belle des formes, qui est l'homme moral ;...Dieu dans l'Homme." *Id.* p. 213. " Il est roi pour longtemps encore...Sa beauté est éternelle, son règne n'aura pas de fin...Tandis qu'un cœur noble aspirera à la beauté morale, tandis qu'une âme élevée tressaillera de joie devant la réalisation du divin, le Christ aura des adorateurs par la partie vraiment éternelle de son être." *Id.* 214. Even Strauss speaks of Him as "the highest object we can possibly imagine with respect to religion, *the Being without whose presence in the mind perfect piety is impossible,*" *Vergängl. und Bleibende in Christenthum,* p. 132. How so, if He *claimed* to be sinless, *claimed* even to be a God, *and was not?* It is, however, delightful thus to see His enemies fall on their knees while they gaze at Him. This awful and transcendent beauty of His Life overawed even the insolent and flippant soul of Voltaire. See the remarkable vision in *Dict. Philosophique,* Art. *Religion.*

"He bids us—when we least expect it
Take back our faith...
Go home and venerate the myth
I thus have experimented with,
This Man, continue to adore Him
Rather than all who went before Him,
And all who ever followed after......"
          Browning, *Christmas Eve and Easter Day.*

the Monks, the pattern of all asceticism; the Philosophers, the enlightener in all truth. To a Fénelon he has seemed the most rapt of mystics; to a Vincent de Paul, the most practical of philanthropists; to an English poet,

> "The best of men
> That ere wore earth about him was a *sufferer*,
> A soft, meek, patient, humble, tranquil spirit,
> *The first true gentleman* that ever breathed [1]."

A sceptical historian, accidentally taking up the New Testament, suddenly finds in Christ the explanation of all History [2]; a fiery demagogue tells a nation, crushed by long oppression, that He was a child of the people, "*le bon sans-culotte* [3];" a victorious Emperor, the last great man of secular History, contrasting his own utter evanescence with Christ's eternal rule, declares that he understands and recognizes men, and that Jesus Christ was not a man [4]; a prophet of anarchy and naturalism, in

[1] Decker.

[2] See a remarkable letter of Johann v. Müller to Karl Bonnet: "In all my study of the ancient times I have always felt the want of something, and it was not till I knew our Lord that all was clear to me; with Him there is nothing that I am not able to solve." Quoted by Luthardt, *Apologet. Vortr.* (Engl. Tr. p. 353.)

[3] Camille Desmoulins. The irreverence of the expression is only in appearance.

[4] Napoleon, in a most remarkable conversation with General Bertrand, repeated by the Comte de Montholon (*Récit de la Captiv. de l'Emp. Napoléon;* see Napoleon, *Table Talk*, Bayard series, pp. 112 sqq.): "I know men, and Jesus Christ is not a man. Superficial minds see a resemblance between Christ and the founder of empires, and the gods of other religions. *That resemblance does not exist. There is between Christ and all other religions whatsoever the distance of infinity;* from the first day to the last He is the same—

F. H. L. 6

the mid confession of his faith, suddenly bursts into eloquent admiration, and "with a hand as firm as that of a martyr," writes that "if the life and death of Socrates are those of a sage, the life and death of Jesus are those of a God."

Yes, the life of Christ is indeed an example, a ὑπογραμμόν[1], over which the loveliest of saints' lives have been but faintly traced; a glory, of which all that is bright among Christians has been but "a pale image and faint reflection[2]." Beautiful indeed has been the life of the saints

always the same, majestic and simple, infinitely firm and infinitely gentle." There is every reason to believe, both from its authentication by competent witnesses and from internal evidence, that the conversation is genuine.

[1] ὑμῖν ὑπολιμπάνων ὑπογραμμόν, ἵνα ἐπακολουθήσητε τοῖς ἴχνεσιν αὐτοῦ, 1 Pet. ii. 21. See other instances in Schleusner, Lex. s. v. It would be indeed a marvel if He who was so meek and lowly should yet have been the only Saint who claimed, both by word and deed, to be free from all sin (John viii. 46). It should be definitely understood that if Christ were *not* sinless and divine, He would be *lower* not *higher* than all who have lived holily on earth; for then His claims would be false, and His personality stained with the poor vice of self-satisfaction. But His sinlessness is beyond all dispute, not only in His entire tone, but even in His prayers, in which there is not the slightest trace of consciousness of sin and petition for forgiveness (see Steinert, *Dissert. de peculiari indole precum Domini*, 1817. Stier, *Reden Jesu*, IV. 427). There are many touches in His individuality which simply could not have been imagined or invented: they bear on the face of them the most certain stamp of historic truth.

[2] τροφέα, πατέρα, διδάσκαλον, σύμβουλον, ἰατρόν, νοῦν, φῶς, τιμήν, δόξαν, ἰσχύν, ζωήν, *Ep. ad Diognet.* c. IX. "O æterna veritas, et vera caritas, et cara æternitas, tu es Deus meus". Aug. "Christ is the Light, let us receive the light; Christ is the Truth, let us believe the truth; Christ is the Way, let us follow the way. And because

of God, and one has been full of charity, and one of purity, and one of zeal; but *this* life is not a type of any one excellence, but a radiation of them all; not virtuous, but Virtue; not truthfulness, but Truth. What mind even of saint or martyr has been large enough, lofty enough, noble enough to comprehend its glorious contradictions,— its clinging friendship and sublime independence, its tender patriotism and humanitarian breadth, its passionate emotion and perfect peace, its unapproachable majesty and childlike sweetness,—the meekness of the Lion of Judah and the wrath of the Lamb that was slain? Even His enemies bore witness to His sinlessness[1]. The

He is our only Master, our only Teacher, our only Shepherd, and chief Captain; therefore let us become His servants, His scholars, His sheep, and His soldiers." *Sermon on the Nativity*, Homilies, II. 12. "The more truly you serve Christ," says Dr Congreve, the Priest of the English Comtists, "the more thoroughly you mould yourselves into His image, the more keen will be your sympathy and admiration."

[1] Even a Francis of Assisi and a Vincent de Paul, and many of the sweetest and purest of the saints, did not escape the pestilent breath of slander; yet, though He lived in familiar intercourse with publicans and harlots, His worst enemies never dared to breathe suspicion on the spotless innocence of Christ. See de Lamennais, *Ess. sur l'Indiff.* IV. p. 201. On the other hand, no heathen ever claimed to be sinless, Soph. *Ant.* 10; Hor. *Sat.* I. 3. 68: Nam *vitiis nemo sine nascitur* optimus ille est Qui minimis nascetur. Εἶναι ἄνδρα ἀγαθὸν ἀδύνατον καὶ οὐκ ἀνθρώπειον, ἀλλὰ θεὸς μόνος τοῦτο ἔχει τὸ γέρας, Simonides. These and other similar passages are quoted by Schneider, *Christliche Klänge aus dem griech. und röm. Klassikern*, 133 sqq.: cf. Cic. *Tusc.* II. 22. In quo vero erit perfecta sapientia (*quem adhuc nos quidem vidimus neminem;* sed philosophorum sententiis, qualis hic futurus sit, si modo aliquando fuerit, exponetur), &c.: and, as the Fathers so often point out, some of the greatest philosophers were personally very base.

Toldoth Jeschu is filled with blasphemies against Him, and yet dare charge Him with no sin save His claim to be the Son of God. "Have thou nothing to do with that just man," said the Roman lady [1]. "I find no fault in this man," witnessed the blood-stained Pilate [2]. "This man hath done nothing amiss [3]," exclaimed the dying malefactor. "I have shed innocent blood [4]," shrieked the miserable Judas. His most eager accusers stammered into self-refuting lies; the witnesses of His uttermost humiliation as they returned smote upon their breasts with despairing agony and assented to the cry of the heathen centurion, "Truly this was the Son of God [5]."

And therefore, not because He was a Prophet and a Teacher so great that He could address even a St Peter and a St John as "my little children [6];" not because He

[1] Matt. xxvii. 19.   [2] Matt. xxvii. 23; Luke xxiii. 14.
[3] Luke xxiii. 40; 1 Pet. ii. 22.   [4] αἷμα ἀθῷον. Matt. xxvii. 4.
[5] Matt. xxvii. 54; Luke xxiii. 47, 48; 1 Cor. i. 19; Heb. vii. 26, 27; 2 Cor. v. 21. &c.
[6] τεκνία ἔτι μικρὸν μεθ᾽ ὑμῶν εἰμι, John xiii. 33; παιδία, *id.* xxi. 16. See the beautiful treatise of Ullmann, *Die Sündlosigkeit Jesu*, pp. 38—71. Christlieb, *Moderne Zweifel*, p. 489. Very few (Weber, Bretschneider, Fritzsche) have been found to deny this ἀναμαρτησία of Christ. Even Strauss admits that "In all those natures which were only purified by struggles and violent disruptions (think only of a Paul, an Augustine, or Luther) the shadowy colour of this remains for ever, and something hard and severe and gloomy clings to them all their lives; but of this in Jesus no trace is found." Strauss indeed ventures to criticise as weakness the agony in the garden, but no Christian will wish that argument should be wasted on such a reproach. The mere fact, however, that the Evangelists, who knew so well how to describe a fearless death (Acts vii.), have described this "weakness"—if Strauss can call it so —of an heroic soul, is an overwhelming argument against the

was *a* Son of God, but because He was *the* Son of God, *therefore* we worship Him. For if, not being divine, He yet claimed divinity, we should shrink back from Him revolted and appalled. The meanest capacity can recognize the unutterable distance which separates man from God; and how could we respect One, who, not being God, yet even in the feebleness of His obscurity, even in the depth of His nameless humiliation, even in the utter impotence of His human infirmity, made Himself equal with God? Oh would not this have been the very blasphemy of imposture, the very insanity of self-deception, the very fatuity of arrogance in one whom all have recognized as the wisest, humblest, holiest of the sons of men? Truly, if we reject His Godhead, then, though we took not up stones to stone Him, we might well turn from Him with agonies of wrath and tears. There is in such a case 'but one step from the Capitol to the Tarpeian rock'; but one step from our adoring devotion to our indignant shame. But because they

---

mythical theory (see Pascal, *Pens.* II. p. 323). Christ's distinct separation of His Sonship from that of all others appears far more clearly in the Greek Testament than in the English version; *e.g.* of His own prayers to God He uses the word ἐρωτᾶν (John xiv. 16, xvi. 26, xvii. 9, 15, 20), "*familiarem petendi modum notat, qualis inter colloquentes solet esse. Sæpius de precibus Jesu occurrit, semel tantum de precibus fidelium.*" Lampe. Again, He says, ἀναβαίνω πρὸς τὸν πατέρα μου from καὶ πατέρα ὑμῶν, John xx. 17, "*I ascend unto the Father of me and Father of you. First* of me and then of you; not therefore *His* because ours, but therefore *ours* because *His.*" Bp. Pearson *on the Creed*, Art. I. "Dicimur et filii Dei, sed ille *aliter* filius Dei." Aug. *on Psalm* lii. Again, men are never bidden ἀγαπᾶν, but φιλεῖν τὸν θεόν, but ὁ πατὴρ φιλεῖ τὸν υἱόν. John v. 20.

believed as we believe, that He was God in the form of a servant, and in the likeness of sinful men, therefore the Jews accepted a martyred Galilean as their Messiah, the Greeks and Romans a crucified Jew as their God, and the fierce northern hordes exchanged their warrior deities for the peaceful suffering humiliation of the White Christ. And what is it that the modern theorists ask us to believe[1]? They ask us to believe that, 1800 years ago, there lived in the most despised village of the most despised province of a conquered land, a man (and here may I be pardoned for that which a Christian may well shudder to repeat)—a man unlearned and ignorant and not free from sin—the son of peasant parents who, after having lived thirty years in the deepest obscurity, as a village carpenter, came forth for three years to preach a doctrine which had no originality, a doctrine which is often self-contradictory, always defective, exaggerated and unpractical, and that when this fantastic pietist, half-dreamer, half-deceiver,

---

[1] See de Lamennais, *Essai sur l'Indifférence*, IV. p. 458. "Que la philosophie est ingénieuse et profonde dans ses conjectures ! Comme les événements qui paraissaient les plus extraordinaires deviennent simples dès qu'elle daigne les expliquer !...Les Apôtres ont dit, Nous vous annonçons l'Évangile au nom de l'Éternel, et vous devez nous croire, car nous sommes doués de pouvoir miraculeux... A ce discours le peuple est accouru de toutes parts, pour être témoin des miracles promis avec tant de confiance. Les malades n'ont point été guéris, les perclus n'ont pas marché, les aveugles n'ont point vu...Alors transporté d'admiration le peuple est tombé aux pieds des Apôtres, et s'est écrié Ceux-ci sont manifestement les envoyés de Dieu !" I am sorry to spoil by abridgement the fine scorn of this magnificent passage.

made claims so violently opposed to His own clearest teachings that He suffered a slave's death for treason and blasphemy, His followers grossly falsified the events of His ordinary life; and though they were men whose lives and teaching showed that they would "*rather die than lie*," yet, suddenly transformed by this utter failure and shameful death from coward fugitives into dauntless missionaries, they either invented or imagined an ignorant story about His resurrection, in attestation of which they were ever ready, with demented enthusiasm, to face the wild beast and stand undaunted in the flame: and that on this empty teaching and this invented tale, was built a Church which, after eighteen centuries, is still invincible in proportion on its purity and its faith; and were founded the institutes of a new kingdom of God, which, "with the unresistible might of weakness," rising up between an effete Judaism and a guilty heathendom, revolutionized and overcame the world. Is there no cleft here, no broad chasm, no unbridgeable abyss, between the real effect and the imaginary cause? Of the Christian consciousness, of the inward witness of the Spirit, of spiritual things being spiritually discerned, of doing the will and so knowing the doctrine, I say nothing[1]: but I ask whether as a mere matter of criticism and history, this whole structure of rationalism does not, at the mere touch of the Gospels, totter before our eyes, and crumble into a vast incongruous

---

[1] "Philosophia veritatem quærit, Theologia invenit, *Religio possidet.*" Pic. Mirand. *Opp.* 359 (Raumer, *Gesch. d. Pädagogik,* t. p. 54).

heap of absurdities and impossibilities[1]? Oh that each one of us, standing on the mound that makes this ruined Babel of false philosophy, even if he have asked with Nathanael, "can any good thing come out of Nazareth?" even if he have said with the unbelieving Jews, "We know this man whence he is;" nay, even if he have doubted as Thomas once doubted; even if he have denied as Peter once denied; yet, feeling at length that "God was in Christ, reconciling the world unto Himself," feeling that in Him his yearnings are satisfied, by Him his sins forgiven, may be enabled to raise his eyes to heaven and exclaim from the depths of an adoring and believing heart,

"*MY LORD AND MY GOD.*"

[1] Really no hypothesis seems too absurd or gratuitous for the exigencies of Rationalism. Comte, for instance, eminent as he is both for the candour, the power, and the historical acuteness of his mind, makes Paul the founder of Christianity, and supposes that *he*—he "the fusile Apostle," he, the α and ω of whose teaching was the *fact* of the Resurrection,—looked out for, and with sublime self-sacrifice subordinated himself to "*one of the many adventurers who were naturally led at that time to attempt the inauguration of Monotheism by aspiring, like their Greek predecessors, at divinisation!!*" He looked out for another, because "he could not give *himself* out for an incarnation of the divine without a mixture of hypocrisy and fanaticism incompatible with real superiority of heart and spirit." He thus, *i.e.*, by merely *propagating* instead of actually *inventing* a falsehood—"saved himself from all personal degradation, and afterwards got really to venerate a type which he idealized." Comte, *Politique Positive*, III. pp. 409, 410. And this is a philosophic view of the origin of Christianity! St Paul, we may be sure, would have wished himself plunged in the lowest abyss of "personal degradation," rather than utter one word capable of any interpretation which should thus blaspheme his Lord.

III.

THE VICTORIES OF CHRISTIANITY.

―――ἴνα μείνῃ τὰ μὴ σαλευόμενα.
Ἐπ. πρὸς Ἑβρ. (xii. 27).

ACTS V. 39.

But if it be of God, ye cannot overthrow it.

MATT. XV. 13.

Every plant, which my heavenly Father hath not planted, shall be rooted up.

1 COR. I. 25.

The foolishness of God is wiser than men, and the weakness of God is stronger than men.

I HAVE ventured, my brethren, to throw together these three passages—uttered, under memorable circumstances by our Blessed Lord, by the wise Rabbi of the Jews, by the great Apostle of the Gentiles—as an authoritative prophecy, as a deeply-seated conviction, as an adequate explanation, of the series of majestic facts, which we shall with God's blessing, pass in review to-day. For having seen the antecedent reasonableness of our Christian faith, and having examined the value of its records, to-day we must consider the evidence of its history; and that evidence—extending as it does over a continuous period of 1800 years—must be to us decisive. Little as the thought may have been familiar to the ancient world, we who accept as indisputable the formula—"*Divinâ Providentiâ agitur mundus et homo*"—with which the Christian Orosius begins his summary of history,—we, who know that God reveals His will not by sudden catastrophes and violent revolutions, but by the steady and secular shining of eternal principles and unhasting laws—we who regard the story of nations as a study scarcely less sacred than Theology itself, because we look on it as a vast drama in which God's purposes towards our race are irresistibly evolved in slow but unbroken sequence,—*we*, I say, must consider the witness of history as decisive respecting the claims of our belief. If its pretensions were fictitious, if its doctrines were erroneous, we should be certain that in the long run it would present a history of decadence and failure, of pernicious influences and inevitable decline; if it be of God, we know beforehand that its course will have been victorious and beneficent,—rising like a Sun of righteousness with healing in its wings. That Sun may be obscured by clouds and storms; its rays may be sometimes hidden by disastrous eclipse or wintry night; but, whether shrouded by temporary darkness or dimmed by passing mist, its light is never quenched; and, breaking forth again from the uttermost part of the heavens, it "runneth about unto the end of it again; and there is nothing hid from the heat thereof[1]."

---

[1] "Cette église qui adore celui qui a toujours été adoré a subsisté sans interruption. Et ce qui est admirable, incomparable, et tout à fait divin, est que cette religion qui a toujours duré a toujours été combattue. *Mille fois elle a été à la veille d'une*

In rudest outline, then, suffer me rapidly to sketch what the progress of Christianity has been, and when you have heard it, judge for your own selves whether men gather grapes from thorns, or figs from thistles; judge whether Error would thus have had a healing influence, and Imposture a regenerative power; and if you believe that there is indeed a Divinity in the affairs of men, judge whether He who is the True, the Faithful, the Righteous, the Unchangeable, would have deceived His own truest children and falsified His own inmost nature, by thus giving blessing to an hallucination, and triumph to a lie!

When that one word[1] was uttered on the Cross which told that the great work was done,—nay, even when the Twelve had seen the risen Christ,—nothing could have appeared more deplorable than the weakness of the new religion. It numbered but a handful of timid followers, of whom the boldest had denied his Lord with blasphemy, and the most devoted had forsaken Him and fled. They were poor, they were ignorant, they were helpless[2]. They could not claim a single synagogue, or a single sword. If they spoke their own language it bewrayed them by its mongrel dialect; if they spoke the

---

destruction universelle ; et toutes les fois qu'elle a été en cet état, Dieu l'a relevée par des coups extraordinaires de sa puissance." Pascal, *Pens.* II. p. 200.

[1] τετέλεσται, John xix. 30.

[2] See the names of contempt heaped upon them by Pagans, *e.g.*, by Cæcilius the Pagan interlocutor in the dialogue of Minucius Felix. See too Arnob. *adv. Gent.* I. 28, 29, II. 5, &c. "hebetes," "stolidi," "fatui," "infausti," "athei," &c.

current Greek, it was despised as a miserable *patois*[1]. And of their two doctrines—the Crucifixion and the Resurrection—the one inspired indignant horror[2], the other unbounded scorn[3]. But when they were weak, then were they strong. They had been consecrated for their mighty work by no earthly chrism; they had been baptised with the Holy Ghost and with fire; each faithless heart had been dilated with celestial courage; each lowly forehead mitred with Pentecostal flame!

Well might they have shuddered at that conspiracy of hatred with which they were confronted. So feeble were they and insignificant, that it would have looked like foolish partiality to prophesy for them the limited existence of a Galilæan sect[4]. Had any one seen Paul the aged as, in all the squalor of poverty and all the emancipation of disease, he sat chained to some coarse soldier in the prætorium at Rome; or that Galilæan fisherman, who, under the shadow of the great Temple of

---

[1] "Sed ab indoctis hominibus et rudibus scripta sunt....Trivialis et sordidus sermo est...Barbarismis, solœcismis obsitæ sunt," &c. Arnob. *adv. Gent.* I. 58, 59. *Non eloquimur magna sed vivimus.* Min. Fel. *Octav.* 8. Ecclesia Christi non de Academiâ et Lycæo, sed de vili plebecula congregata est. Jerome, *Com. in. Ep. ad. Gal.* III. 3.

[2] Arnob. *adv. Gent.* I. 36, 40. ἀποδείκνυμεν οὐ λόγον καθαρὸν καὶ ἅγιον ἀλλὰ ἄνθρωπον ἀτιμότατον καὶ ἀποτυμπανισθέντα, Orig. *c. Cels.* II. 31.

[3] *Id.* II. 8.

[4] This may partly be the reason for the all but total silence of the Jewish writers. It is, however, probable that the celebrated passage of Josephus, *Ant.* XVIII. 4, is not so much *spurious* as largely *interpolated.* See Salvador, *Jésus Christ et sa Doctrine,* I. 157. Jahn, *Hebr. Commonwealth,* § 125.

Artemis, ministered to a handful of poor converts in the splendid capital of Asia,—would it not have seemed the very fanaticism of credulity to prophesy that their names should be honoured for ever by the inhabitants of cities more magnificent than Ephesus, and empires more vast than Rome? St. Paul died; they dragged, it may be, his corpse from the arena, and—sprinkling the white dust over the stains of his feeble blood—looked for a more interesting victim than the aged and nameless Jew; St John died we know not where or how, and no memorial marks his forgotten tomb[1]; yet, to this day, over the greatest of modern cities towers the vast dome of the cathedral dedicated to the name of Paul; and the shapeless mounds which once were Ephesus bear witness, in their name of Agiotzeologo, to no other fact than that they once were trodden by the weary feet of him who saw the Apocalypse, and whose young head had rested on the bosom of his Lord!

Consider how colossal were the powers arrayed against this nascent faith[2],—how vast the forest-trees

---

[1] "Das Andenken an Johannes wird (nach Tournefort) noch in dem Namen des Ortes *Ajasoluk* erhalten, welcher aus ἅγιος θεόλογος (Seologos von den Griechen gesprochen) corrumpirt ist." Winer, *Bibl. Realwört.* s. v. Ephesus. Fellowes, however (*Exc. in Asia Minor*), and Arundell (*Seven Churches*) derive it from a Turkish root, meaning City of the Moon, certainly on no convincing grounds.

[2] "Tout ce qu'il y a de grand sur la terre s'unit, les savants, les sages, les rois, les uns écrivent, les autres condamnent, les autres tuent. Et nonobstant toutes ces oppositions, ces gens simples et sans force résistent à toutes ces puissances...et ôtent l'idolâtrie de toute la terre." Pascal, *Pens.* II. 319. ed. Faugère. "Coming to set right and to govern the world, it has ever been, as it ought to be, in

which overshadowed with their dense umbrage, and well-nigh crushed under their deciduous leaves, this smallest of all seeds. First, Judaism both within and without the fold. Judaism *within*,—half suggesting to the minds of more than one Apostle that, unless they conformed to its outward observances, they were little better than a schismatic sect ; Judaism *without*, with its fifteen hundred years of gorgeous worship and holy faith. The Jewish Rabbi—such a one as he into whose mouth Celsus has placed some of his bitterest rebukes—might, with plausibility, taunt them as traitorous apostates, as he recalled to some young proselyte that long and splendid history, rolling back from the heroic Asmonæan struggles to the magnificence of Solomon,—nay, backward to the day when, with uplifted spear, Joshua had bidden the sun to stand still upon Gibeon, and Abraham, obeying the mysterious summons, had abandoned the gods of his fathers in Ur of the Chaldees. The rod of Moses, the harp of David, the ephod of Samuel, the mantle of Elijah, the graven gems on Aaron's breast,—all these were theirs ; theirs, too, the granite tables of Sinai, theirs the living oracles of God ; and who were these children of yesterday, these miserable Galilæans with their crucified Nazarene, in whom none of the rulers or the Pharisees had believed ? were they not beneath contempt ? a people that " knew not the law," and were accursed ?

conflict with great masses of men, with the civil power, with physical force, with adverse philosophies ; it has had successes, it has had reverses, but it has had a grand history, and has effected great things, and is as vigorous in its age as in its youth." Newman, *Gram. of Assent* p. 425.

It needed no mean force of character, no ordinary intensity of conviction,—it needed, let us say, the divine vision of a Peter, and the inspired eloquence of a Paul, to burst the intolerable yoke of these long-venerated observances, and to plant the standard of Christian freedom upon the ruins of Levitical form[1]. And Jews as they were by birth, Jews as they were in great measure by religion, keeping as they did the Jewish Sabbath, worshipping in the Jewish Temple, venerating the Jewish books, the struggle against Jewish detestation might have been far longer and more terrible but for a Divine interposition. Forty years after the imprecation of priests and people, the blood of the King whom they had crucified fell like a rain of fire from heaven upon them and on their children[2]. The storm of Roman invasion consumed Jerusalem to ashes, and shook the whole fabric of Judaism into the dust. The race became despised and persecuted, wanderers with the brand

---

[1] Acts xv. 10; Gal. v. 1.

[2] "Dispersi, palabundi, et cœli et soli sui extorres vagantur per orbem sine nomine, sine Deo," &c. Tert. *adv. Jud.* 15. See a passage of terrible and almost savage power in De Lamennais: "Peuple incompréhensible, cesse un moment le travail dont tu te consumes sous le soleil, rassemble-toi des quatre vents, où le souffle de Dieu t'a dispersé, viens et réponds...Juif, tu n'as pas fait en vain cette demande (*que son sang soit sur nous et sur nos enfants*), ton souhait est accompli, le sang est sur toi, il y sera toujours, va, retourne à ton supplice, que le monde entier en soit témoin jusqu'au jour, où réconnaissant et détestant ton crime, ce sang, ce même sang que tu as versé l'effacera." *Ess. sur l'Indifférence*, IV. p. 199 It is said that a chaplain of Frederic William I. of Prussia, having been ordered to give the briefest possible proof of the truth of Christianity, replied, "The Jews, your Majesty."

of God upon their brow. The frantic hatred of a false Messiah at length taught the Pagan world that Christians were something more than a Jewish[1] sect; but when Bether had been taken, and Akiba slain in prison, and Barkokeba had fallen before the sword of Julius Severus[2], the material power of the Jews, and therewith the main hopes of the Semitic race, were broken for ever; and, without an effort of its own, the first great obstacle to the spread of Christianity had been irrevocably swept sway.

II. Harder, deadlier, more varied, more prolonged was the contest of Christianity with Paganism. From the first burst of hatred in the Neronian persecution till the end of the third century the fierce struggle continued; fierce, because—meek, unobtrusive, spiritual, as the Christians were—they yet roused the hatred of every single class. Paganism never troubled itself to be angry with mere philosophers who aired their elegant doubts in the shady xystus or at the luxurious feast, but who with cynical *insouciance* did what they detested, and adored what they despised. They were unworthy of that corrosive hatred which is[3] the tribute

[1] Afterwards the Christians were contemptuously called "*genu tertium*," or nondescript body.

[2] See Jahn, *Hebr. Commonwealth*, Eng. Tr. p. 196. He was afterwards called Bar Koziba (בַּר כּוֹזִיבָא) "son of lie."

[3] Had the Christians even remotely countenanced the prevalent spirit of eclecticism they might have received very different treatment, as may be seen from the story that the Emperor Alexander Severus admitted an image of Christ into his lararium. Similar stories, but more improbable, are told of Tiberius and Hadrian. Tert. *Apolog.* 20; Euseb. *Hist. Ecc.* II. 2; Kaye, *Eccl. Hist.* p. III;

paid to the simplicity of Virtue by the despair and
agony of Vice. But these Christians, who turned away
with aversion from temples and statues, who refused to
witness the games of the amphitheatre, who would die
rather than fling into the altar-flame a pinch of incense
to the genius of the Emperors [1]; who declined even to
wear a garland of flowers at the banquet, or pour a
libation at the sacrifice [2]; whose austere morality was a
terrible reflection on the favourite sins which had eaten,

Lamprid. *Vit. Alex. Sev.* 29. See Gibbon, I. 570 (Milman, ed.).
Pyrrho, although an open and notorious Atheist, had died a priest of
Elis. Augustine, after quoting a fragment of Seneca, in which he
says that philosophers, as a matter of indifference, will worship all
that ignoble crowd of gods which long superstition has accumulated,
adds, " *Colebat quod reprehendebat, agebat quod arguebat, quod culpa-
bat adorabat*," *De Civ. Dei*, VI. 10. The same general indifference
characterises the dead selfishness of modern sceptics; to them
applies what Plutarch says of the Epicurean: " He hypocritically
enacts prayer for fear of the many; he utters words directly
opposed to his philosophy. While he sacrifices, the ministering
priest seems to him no more than a cook, and he departs uttering
the line of Menander: 'I have sacrificed to the gods in whom I
have no concern.'" Voltaire's characteristic excuse was: "Il y a des
gens qui craignent des araignées, il y en a d'autres qui les avalent."

[1] Tert. *Apolog.* 29—34, *passim.*

[2] *Id. De Corona Militis*, and *De Spectaculis*, passim. Only those
who are ignorant of what Christianity was, and what battle it had to
fight, can join Gibbon in sneering at their resolute determination to
break with Paganism; see Kaye, *Eccl. Hist.* p. 389. "Nihil est nobis
dictu, visu, auditu *cum insaniâ circi, cum impudicitiâ theatri
cum atrocitate arenæ, cum vanitate xysti*." Tert. *Apol.* 38. "Non
spectacula visitis, non pompis interestis ..*non floribus caput nectitis*,
non corpus odoribus honestatis...pallidi, misericordia digni et
nostrorum deorum." Minuc. Fel. *Oct.* 8. "Latebrosa et lucifuga
natio, in publicum muta, in angulis garrula." *Id.* 12.

like a spreading cancer, into the very heart of the nation's life; these Christians, with their unpolished barbarism, their unphilosophic ignorance [1], their stolid endurance, their detestable purity, their intolerable meekness, kindled against themselves alike the philosophers whose pride they irritated, the priests whose gains they diminished, the mob whose indulgences they thwarted, the Emperors whose policy they disturbed [2]. Yet, unaided by any, opposed by all, Christianity won. Without one earthly weapon she faced the legionary masses, and, tearing down their adored eagles, replaced them by the sacred monogram of her victorious labarum; she made her instrument of a slave's agony a symbol more glorious than the laticlave of consuls or the diadem of kings; without eloquence she silenced the subtle dialectics of the Academy, and without knowledge the encyclopædic ambition of the porch. The philosopher who met a Christian Bishop on his way to the Council of Nicæa, stammered into a confession of belief, and

---

[1] "*Indoctis, impolitis, rudibus, agrestibus*, quibus non est datum intelligere civilia, multo magis denegatum est disserere divina." Minuc. Fel. *Oct*. 12. βάρβαρον δόγμα. Aug. *c. Cels*. I. 12. βάρβαρος φιλοσοφία. Tatian, *Apol*. 20.

[2] St Augustine has most powerfully expressed the deadliest causes of this hatred, which lay in the check given by Christianity to the favourite vices of the heathens, *De Civ. Dei*, II. 20. μισεῖ καὶ χριστιανοὺς ὁ κόσμος μηδὲν ἀδικούμενος ὅτι ταῖς ἡδοναῖς ἀντιτάσσονται. *Ep. ad Diognet*. VI. See a beautiful passage to the same effect in the *Protreptikon* of Clemens: φεύγωμεν ὦ συνναῦται, φεύγωμεν τὸ κῦμα τοῦτο, πῦρ ἐρεύγεται, νῆσός ἐστι πονηρά, ὀστοῖς καὶ νεκροῖς σεσωρευμένη, ᾄδει δὲ ἐν αὐτῇ πορνίδιον ὡραῖον, ἡδονή...*Protrept*. XI. 2. § 118.

the last of Pagan Emperors died prematurely in the wreck of his broken powers, with the despairing words, "Vicisti Galilæe!" "Oh Galilæan[1], thou hast conquered!"

i. In its terrror and hatred, Paganism essayed a *triple* resistance. First, it tried the experiment of an ec'ectic revival. For the old humanistic worship, with its frank and sunny anthropomorphism, it substituted a naturalistic cult, which, for an age of decaying faith, had a horrible fascination. From Egypt it imported the imposing mysteries of Isis; from Persia the worship of Mithras, with its painful initiations and ritual splendour; from Phrygia the orgiastic rites of Cybele with their brutal mutilations and nameless infamies[2]. And this Neopaganism, welded out of archaic superstitions, inspired the most frenzied enthusiasm by appealing to the most degraded tastes. But the revival, with all its paraphernalia of mathematicians and jugglers, lustrations and oracles, weird exorcisms and ghastly taurobolia, was all in vain; it never succeeded in galvanising into even the

---

[1] Julian had ordered that the Christians should be always called Galilæans, and forbade the instruction of their children in classic literature. Socrates, II. 16, Theodoret. III. 8.

[2] Among other rites were the disgusting taurobolium and criobolium, which marked, as Gieseler says, "the extreme sensuality of superstition;" see Döllinger, *The Gentile and the Jew* (tr. Darvell), II. p. 179. In this learned, but very painful book, may be found a full account of the Eclectic Revival of Paganism; as also in De Pressensé, *Hist. des Trois Prem. Siècles*, II. 1—60; Neander, *Church History* (E. T.) I. pp. 14—18, 40—43, &c.; Gieseler, *Compend.* § 37 (E. T. I. 47), &c.

semblance of life the corrupting corpse of the old religion. Great Pan was dead [1].

ii. Then, secondly, they tried the experiment of argument [2]. Lucian, in his *Peregrinus*, which is a travesty of martyrdom, and his *Philopseudes*, which is a parody on miracles, confronted them with his degrading laughter and Epicurean sneer [3]. Philostratus in his life of Apollonius [4], Jamblichus in his life of Pythagoras, tried to emulate their gospels with the false miracles of a late sophist and an antique philosopher. Porphyry and Hierocles met them with haughty mysticism and intellectual theosophy. Celsus opened upon them the battering violence of his impassioned rhetoric. But on this field, too, Christianity matched them. It repelled argument with argument; it repaid scorn with scorn [5].

[1] Πὰν ὁ μέγας τέθνηκε. See the strange and beautiful story of the grammarian Epithyrsis told by Plut. *De Orac. Defectu*, alluded to in Milton's *Ode to the Nativity*, and on which Mrs Barrett Browning has founded her beautiful poem.

[2] Neander, *Ch. Hist.* II. 214 seqq. E. Tr.

[3] It would be difficult to name any writer more hopelessly, essentially, cynically immoral than Lucian. He is the type of atheistic selfishness. He believes in nothing and no one; "men please him not, nor women neither." Evaporating from heathen mythology both its poetry and its imaginativeness, he leaves it hideously bare. He contemplates not the loveliness or the sorrows of Helen, but her skull; not the courage or generosity of Achilles, but his rage and lust. He reminds us of Tennyson's Vivienne, whose tongue
"Ran fire at will among the noblest names."

[4] "Apollonius demeure toujours *le Christ d'eclecticisme panthéiste*, de la gnose orientale, la flottante personnification de ses rêves variés et indécis." De Pressensé, *Hist. des Trois Prem. Siècles*, II. p. 148.

[5] Bunsen, *Gott in der Gesch.* v. p. 5.

THE VICTORIES OF CHRISTIANITY. 103

Sarcasm and invective were indeed unchristian implements, which the Apologists had better have disdained to wield : yet the *Raillery of Philosophers* by Hermias was full of delicate irony, and even Pagan hatred never surpassed the pitiless denunciations of Tatian, the concentrated anger of Arnobius, the deep gloom and scorching glare of the intense Tertullian. But far better and nobler than these were the lofty Apologies of the Alexandrian Fathers, who by their breadth and profundity wrought for the Church an imperishable service. It was well indeed that a Celsus and a Porphyry could be matched with such noble specimens of spiritual intuition and exhaustive learning as the *Protreptikon* of a Clemens, and the eight books of an Origen [1]. Models for the best and most Christian school of controversy, they refute indeed the calumnies of their opponents ; but, better than this, for each refuted error they offer a beautiful and convincing truth ; and, recognizing the divine spark which glimmered even in the white embers of heathen wisdom, summon their adversaries to drink with them of the living fountain, and share with them the Eternal Light [2]. Man was to them no " warped slip of

[1] It should be a warning to the Church that this most memorable of all the *Apologies*, ancient and modern, was written by one who was under the ban of excommunication ! See De Pressensé, *Hist. de l'Église*, II. p. 364.

[2] What a fine passage is that in S. Clemens of Alexandria summoning the blind Tiresias of heathendom to gaze with him upon the living light : σπεῦσον Τειρεσία, πίστευσον, ὄψει· Χριστὸς ἐπιλάμπει φαιδρότερον ἡλίου, δι' ὃν ὀφθαλμοὶ τυφλῶν ἀναβλέπουσιν, νύξ σε φεύξεται...ὄψει τοὺς οὐρανούς, ὦ γέρον, ὁ Θήβας μὴ βλέπων. *Protrept.* XII. § 119.

wilderness," but a φυτὸν οὐράνιον, "a heavenly plant;" and in every heathen inscription their enlightened eye read a prayer to the Unknown God. Neither Stoicism, with its unnatural apathy and utter hopelessness[1], nor Neoplatonism with its cold Pantheism and esoteric pride, had a chance against these living and loving truths. The *Enchiridion* of Epictetus, the *Meditations* of Aurelius are full of beautiful counsel, yet they are too sad and too weak to reach the multitude or even to sway the few; and as for the *Enneads* of Plotinus, and the *Commentaries* of *Proclus*, with all their gorgeous invocations and voluminous mysticism, they have ever been to mankind but as the small dust of the balance compared to one verse of the Sermon on the Mount[2].

iii. But, though argument and philosophy failed, though revivals and eclecticism failed, Pagans might

---

[1] The sentiment,
"Know that whatever thou hast been,
'Tis something better not to be,"
is a common one in philosophic literature, Bunsen, *Gott in der Gesch.* v. p. 9. Some quotations from Marcus Aurelius in my *Seekers after God*, pp. 301, 308, will show the English reader the deep sadness of the later Stoicism. See *Id.* pp. 49—51.

[2] It is strange and sad to know that during the reign of Julian all social advance was checked. "Parmi les nombreuses constitutions émanées de Julien, et recueillies par le code Théodosien— *il n'en est pas une seule* qui s'associe au mouvement d'émancipation du droit naturel et de l'équité. Tant il est vrai que le christianisme était désormais le mobile des grandes améliorations sociales." Troplong, *De l'infl. du Christian. sur le Droit Civil*, p. 128. Strauss might have been supposed to sympathize with Julian, but in his life of him he says "dass seine Ideale rückwarts liegen, dass er das Rad der Geschichte rückwarts zu drehen unternimmt."

always rely for victory upon brute force and crushing violence. Even Nero had driven through the gardens of his Golden House between lines of torches of which each one was a martyr in his shirt of fire [1]; but Nero's assault was as nothing in extent or virulence compared with those of a Decius or a Diocletian [2]. Christianity spent her first three centuries in one long, legalized, almost unbroken persecution. Some of her holiest bishops—an Ignatius, a Polycarp, an Hippolytus; some of her greatest writers—a Justin, an Athanasius, an Origen; even her poor female slaves—a Blandina, a Felicitas, a Potamiæna, endured the rack or the prison, perished by the sword or flame. "Yet they stood safe," said Cyprian, "stronger than their conquerors; the beaten and lacerated members conquered the beating and lacerating hooks [3]." "The nearer I am to the sword," said Ignatius [4], "the nearer to God." "We were condemned to the wild beasts," wrote the youthful St Perpetua, "and with hearts full of joy returned

---

[1] The "tunica molesta," or "incendialis." See Juv. *Sat.* I. 155, VIII. 235; Tert. *adv. Nat.* I. 18; *Ad Mart.* 5, &c.

[2] See Cave, *Prim. Christianity*, II. ch. vi. vii.

[3] The ungulæ were "a kind of iron pincers, made with sharp teeth, with which the flesh was by piecemeal pulled and torn off their backs." Cave, *Prim. Christianity*, II. 7. One was found in the Vatican cemetery. *Rom. Subter.* II. 4, p. 149. Prudentius calls them "bisulcæ." Περὶ στεφ. I. 44. See other passages in Forcellini, s. v.

[4] *Ep. ad Smyrn.* 4. The reader will be reminded of the remarkable ἄγραφον δόγμα attributed to our Lord ὁ ἐγγύς μου ἐγγὺς τοῦ πυρός. Dr Newman has finely translated another passage of Ignatius in his *Grammar of Assent*, p. 472.

to our prison !'" "Call us," said the fervent Tertullian, "call us *Sarmenticii* and *Semaxii*, names derived from the wood wherewith we are burned, and the stakes to which we are bound; this is the garment of our victory, our embroidered robe, our triumphal chariot [2]." Such was their "tremendous spirit;" and when the very executioners were weary, when vast holocausts had been offered to the expiring divinities, then finding, as has been finely said, that she had to deal with "a host of Scævolas," 'the proudest of earthly powers arrayed in the plenitude of material resources humbled herself before a power founded on a mere sense of the unseen [3].'

Yes, it was of God, and they could not overthrow it[4]:

[1] *Acta SS. Perpetuæ et Felicitatis* (which are referred to by Tert. *De Anima*, 55.). For an account of their martyrdom, see Alban Butler, *Lives of the Saints*, March 7. The reader will be reminded of "magis damnati quam absoluti gaudemus," Tert. *Ad Scap.* 1.

[2] "Licet nunc sarmenticios et semaxios appelletis, quia ad stipitem dimidii axis revincti sarmentorum ambitu exurimur. Hic est habitus victoriæ nostræ, hæc palmata vestis, tali curru triumphamus," Tert. *Apolog.* § 50. And again "Si denotatur gloriatur; si accusatur non defendit; interrogatus vel ultro confitetur; damnatus gratias agit," *Id.* § 1. In fact the "martyrii prærogativa" is one of his favourite subjects, *Adv. Valent.* 4; *De Resur. Carnis*, 43; *Scorpiace*, 12, and *passim*. "The angels of martyrdom and victory are brothers," &c. says Mazzini (*Works*, VI. p. 746), "both extend their protecting wings over the cradle of future life."

[3] Newman, *Grammar of Assent*, 472. See the grand conclusion of Mr Browning's *Instans Tyrannus*.

[4] Christianity was never stronger than when Diocletian and Galerius symbolised it on their medals as a strangled hydra with the haughty inscription *Deletâ Christianâ religione*. Two such inscriptions have been found at Clunia, in Spain, on one of which are the words "*Nomine Christianorum deleto qui rempublicam evertebant.*"

the catacomb triumphed over the Grecian temple; the Cross of shame over the wine-cup and the Salian banquet, the song of the siren and the wreath of rose. These obscure sectaries,—barbarians, orientals, Jews as they were,—fought against the indignant world and won. "Not by power, nor by might, but by My Spirit, saith the Lord of hosts;" by heroic endurance, by stainless innocence, by burning zeal, by inviolable truthfulness, by boundless love [1]. The world's seductive ideals and intoxicating joys, the world's enchanting mythologies and dissolute religions—young Dionysus,

> "As he burst upon the East
> A jocund and a welcome conqueror,
> And Aphrodite, sweet as from the sea
> She rose, and floated in her pearly shell
> A laughing girl—"

all fled before a Cross of wood! Yes, my brethren, because that Cross was held by the bleeding hands of the world's true King, who perfected the strength of His

---

Gruter, *Inscript.* p. 210; Lardner, *Credibility*, VII. 548. It is usual, with Augustine, to count ten persecutions (*De Civ. Dei*, XVII. 52; Sulpic. Sev. *Hist.* II. 33), but only *eight* can really be made out; viz. those of Nero (A.D. 64), Trajan (110), Marcus Aurelius (177), Sept. Severus (194), Maximin (238), Decius (249), Valerian (257), Diocletian (303). De Pressensé, *Hist. des Trois Prem. Siècles*, I. p. 297. The firmness of the Christians under torture both amazed and disgusted the Stoics. The jealousy with which they viewed it finds its echo in Lucian's *Peregrinus*, and the μὴ κατὰ ψιλὴν παράταξιν ὡς οἱ Χριστίανοι, which is the only notice taken of them by Marcus Aurelius, XI. 3.

[1] This subject has been magnificently developed by De Lamennais, *Ess. sur l'Indifférence.* "For 300 years spirit struggled against the brutality of sense, the conscience against despotism,

followers in weakness; and, having been lifted up, drew all men unto Him.

III. But worse trials remained. It was a Divine Providence which ordained that, not till after three centuries of unaided struggle, victorious not because of princes, but in spite of them,—when Diocletian had retired smitten with a vague disease, and Galerius, eaten of worms, had revoked his cruel edicts[1], and Maximin, terrified by famine and pestilence, had restored their plundered goods, and Licinius and Maxentius had perished miserably in prison or in battle,—that the terrified world flung itself at the feet of the oppressed, and Christianity mounted the imperial throne. It did not succeed because Constantine became a Christian, but Constantine became a Christian because it had succeeded[2]. Long before the battles of Adrianople or the Milvian bridge, Christianity had carried the day. "We are but of yesterday," said Tertullian, "and we have filled all that belongs to you—the cities, the fortresses, the free towns, the very camps, the palace, the senate, the

---

the soul against the body, virtue against all the vices...Everywhere Christians fell, and everywhere they triumphed." Napoleon, *Table Talk*, p. 18. "Athènes et Rome l'adoptèrent, les barbares tombèrent à ses pieds; et aujourd'hui encore le rationalisme n'ose le regarder un peu fixement qu'à genoux devant lui. Quel qu'il ait été, sa fortune a été plus étonnante encore que lui-même." Renan, *Et. d'Hist. Rel.* 198.

[1] Lactant. *De Mort. Persec.* XXXIV.

[2] See some excellent remarks of De Pressensé, *Hist. des Trois Prem. Siècles*, II. p. 524. "Il fallait que la religion nouvelle fût bien décidément alors le soleil levant, pour qu'un homme comme Constantin s'inclinât devant elle." Cf. I. p. 296.

forum; we leave to you the temples only[1]." Little, indeed, did Christianity owe to that trimming Emperor and unbaptized catechumen,—that strange Christian indeed!—who placed his own bust on the statues of Apollo, who thought the nails of the true Cross a fitting ornament for the bridle of his charger, and on whose extraordinary figure the robes so besmeared with gold and crusted with jewels, could not conceal the Neronian stains of a son's and a consort's blood[2]. But it was in this the supreme hour of her external triumph that the Church was attacked in a new form, by the growth of heresies which threatened more effectually than any persecution to sap her very existence. The rival religion of Mani

---

[1] "Hesterni sumus et vestra omnia implevimus, urbes, insulas, castella, municipia, conciliabula, castra ipsa, tribus, decurias, palatium, senatum ipsum; sola vobis reliquimus templa." Tert. *Apol.* 37. "Tanta multitudo, pars pœne major civitatis." Id. *Ad Scapulam*, 5.

[2] "De Maistre a fait très bien sentir que dans la célèbre transiation à Bysance, Constantin ne fuyait pas moins moralement devant l'Eglise que politiquement devant les Barbares." Comte, *Phil. Pos.* v. 363. Constantine made the very futile attempt to serve two masters. In the same year he published two decrees, of which one commanded the observance of Sunday, and the other directed the consultation of aruspices. Troplong, *De l'Influence du Christianisme sur le Droit Civil*, p. 7. In judging of Constantine, it is impossible not to believe that Zosimus and Julian were nearer the truth than Eusebius. Never perhaps was there a more bitter satire than that written on Constantine ἰσαπόστολος (surely the strangest saint even in the Greek calendar!) by his prime minister Ablavius:—

"Saturni aurea sæcla quis requirat
Sunt hæc *gemmea* sed Neroniana."

Sidon. Apollinar. v. S. See Gibbon, II. 6S (ed. Milman).

with its Zoroastrian doctrines, the long succession of Gnostics with their notions from the Jewish Cabbala and oriental fancy, could hardly be said to disturb her inward peace. The fierce schism of the Donatists, stained as it was with the intolerant fury of the *circumcelliones*, had been mainly confined to a single province. But it is now that we hear for the first time that fatal name of Arianism, which for centuries kindled the most unquenchable hatred in the Church's bosom. The ominous discussions of Patripassians and Sabellians had already prepared the way for the wider heresy of the Alexandrian presbyter. There is no more humiliating period in Christian History. Even an orthodox Christian historian, Socrates [1], compares these frenzied controversies about the Homoousion to a night battle, in which the combatants could neither see each other nor understand. Yet, even in this dark period, we may admire the venerable charity of Hosius of Cordova, the splendid faithfulness of Athanasius the Great. Arianism might infect the court [2], and invade the camp, but it was never

---

[1] Νυκτομαχίας δὲ οὐδὲν ἀπεῖχε τὰ γιγνόμενα, οὔτε γὰρ ἀλλήλους ἐφαίνοντο νοοῦντες ἀφ' ὧν ἀλλήλους βλασφημεῖν ὑπελάμβανον. Socrates, c. 23 (quoted by Dean Milman, *Hist. of Christianity*, II. p. 369). The most significant comment on this fact is ther emark of St Jerome, "vel certe antequam in Alexandria quasi Demonium meridianum Arius nasceretur, *innocenter quædam et minus caute locuti sunt*, et quæ non possint perversorum hominum calumnias declinare." *Apol.* 2, *contr. Ruff.* See Daillé, *On the Right Use of the Fathers*, ch. v.

[2] The partiality of kings for Arianism rose from their instinctive sense that it necessarily involved the diminution of sacerdotal authority, and destroyed the independence of the spiritual from the

true, except in semblance, that Athanasius was alone against the world. There were thousands of knees that had not bowed to Baal, and mouths that had not kissed him. The great heart of the Christian multitude was sound [1]. Amid the unintelligible precision of theological technicalities, which professed to define the indefinable, their instinct told them that the various heresiarchs were taking away their Lord. And meanwhile the defeat of Arianism shows that the Divinity of Christ was no new dogma which had crept unchallenged into the Christian faith; but that, although denied by men of powerful intellects in the highest places, it was yet by the Catholic Church deliberately accepted, solemnly affirmed. At *four* great councils, against *four* great heresies, the Church promulgated her *four* great formulæ on the existence of her Lord—ἀληθῶς, τελέως, ἀδιαιρέτως, ἀσυγχύτως—truly, perfectly, indivisibly, distinctly—truly God, perfectly man, indivisibly God and man, distinctly God and man [2].

IV. Then arose a fresh danger from without. It might well have been thought that in the wild storm of northern barbarian invasion the Church must perish.

temporal power; see Comte, *Pol. Pos.* v. p. 383. "Les historiens catholiques ont justement noté que toutes les hérésies de quelque importance, se trouvaient habituellement accompagnées de graves aberrations morales ou politiques." Id. 387.

[1] Newman, *Grammar of Assent*, p. 479.
[2] δύο φυσικὰς θελήσεις ἤτοι θελήματα ἐν Χριστῷ καὶ δύο φυσικὰς ἐνεργείας ἀδιαιρέτως, ἀτρέπτως, ἀμερίστως, ἀσυγχύτως...κηρύττομεν. *Acta Conc. Const.* (in Dorner, *Entwickelungsgesch. der Lehre von der Person Christ.* p. 103, ed. 1839). Every one will remember the beautiful passage of Hooker, *Eccles. Polit.* Bk. v. liv. 10.

But it was not so written in the book of God's Providence. Those hero-hearts, refined by a true faith, were the necessary basis for modern civilization [1]. The Church's attitude toward them is best symbolized by those majestic scenes in which the violence of Attila the Hun was overawed by Leo III. at Ponte Molino, and of Genseric the Vandal at the gates of Rome [2]. Already they had heard the name of Christ; already courageous missionaries had penetrated their savage forests and traversed their gloomy hills; and thus the fury of their onset was softened by the recognition of virtues more elevated than courage, and blessings more to be desired than strength. And thus Christianity was not only saved, but became herself the bulwark of all that was valuable in the ancient civilizations. When the degenerate Romans had melted down the statue of Virtus [3] to pay their ransom to Alaric, her bishops earned the title of *Defensores Civitatis* [4]. She saved the van-

[1] Comte, *Phil. Pos.* v. p. 401.

[2] "Awed by his majesty the savage who came to plunder and slay abandoned his purpose...; and Totila himself listened patiently to the rebukes and predictions of Benedict." Cox, *Lat. and Teut. Christianity*, p. 137. "The progress of Christianity has been marked by two glorious and decisive victories over the learned and luxurious civilization of the Roman Empire, and over the warlike barbarians of Scythia and Germany, who subverted the Empire, and embraced the religion of the Romans." Gibbon, III. pp. 358 sqq. (ed. Milman).

[3] Zosimus, *Hist.* v. 38. This is one of those ironical and typical accidents (?) of which history is, to every observant eye, so full.

[4] *e.g.*, at Carthage. "It was they," said Mr Mill (and I purposely quote testimonies that will be unsuspected of any bias), "who treated with the invaders in the name of the natives; it was

quished from extirpation, the victors from decay. Barbarians who had seen such types of noble excellence as an Ulphilas or a Severinus, or in later times a Boniface or an Olaf, saw in the priesthood an institution for which they felt a genuine reverence; and this veneration was the means of fusing all that was valuable in two violently conflicting elements into one splendid, permanent, and progressive society. The churches of Christian Rome, built out of the marble of heathen temples, which had been levelled by barbarian hands, are at once a history and a symbol of the work which the Church did for the world[1]."

V. One more external danger, and one alone remained—the sudden and overwhelming growth of Mo-

their adhesion which guaranteed the general obedience; and after the conversion of the conquerors, it was to their sacred character that the conquered were indebted for whatever mitigation they experienced of the fury of conquest." *Dissertations*, II. p. 243. "In the face of the brute force of the corrupt and tottering Empire," says Mazzini, "whose frontiers echoed to the threatening footsteps of the barbarians, those Bishops raised the banner of a moral idea, of a spiritual power, destined to win over the barbarians to its rule." *Fortnightly Rev.*, June, 1870. See too Comte, *Phil. Pos.* VI. ch. 9, which is full of just and noble thoughts.

[1] Ozanam, *Hist. of Civilization in the Fifth Century* (Eng. Tr.), I. p. 14, also Vol. II. chap. vi., in which he shows how much the world is indebted to the happy inspiration—miscalled optimism by those who knew it not—which enabled the Church to abstain from declaring herself menacingly and absolutely against the barbarians, and "enables her to regard those difficult times with a firm and calm glance," and distinguish "the real property of the past amidst the trembling destinies of the future." II. p. 170 seqq. "*Two nations* owed to Gregory the Great *their faith, and with it their civilization.*" Cox, *Lat. and Teut. Christianity*, p. 140.

hammedanism. On religious grounds, indeed, the Church of Christ had nothing—and less than nothing—to fear. Strong only as a military theocracy, Islam as a creed was a mixture of fatal apathy with sensual hopes, and did but repeat the same mechanical formulæ with lips of death[1]. Checked in Europe by a long line of Christian heroes from Charles Martel to John Hunniades, and from Hunniades to Sobieski, its aggressive power was broken. It now acts only as a gradual decay in every nation over which it dominates. The traveller in Palestine may be shocked to see even the fair hill of Nazareth surmounted by the white-domed wely of an obscure Mohammedan saint[2]; but he will be reassured as he notices that in every town and village where Christians are there is activity and vigour, while all the places which are purely Islamite look as though they had been smitten, as with the palsy, by some withering and irreparable curse.

VI. From this time forward Christianity had no external enemy to fear. From the 5th to the 13th century, the Church was engaged in elaborating the most

[1] Mohammedanism, when considered as following Christianity, is a mere anachronism and retrogression; besides which it contained absolutely nothing original. Mohammed had, in his youth, lived much with Jews; the very name *Koran* is borrowed from the Biblical title *mikra*, 'reading,' and it is very largely indebted both to the Pentateuch and the *Talmud*. See Salvador, *Jésus Christ et sa Doctrine*, I. p. 288; Herzog, *Realencycl.* XVIII. 815. "We think Islam neither more nor less than Judaism adapted to Arabia, plus the apostleship of Jesus and Mahomet." Dr Deutsch, Art. *Islam*, in *Quarterly Review*, Vol. CXXVII. No. 254.

[2] Neby Ismail.

splendid organization which the world has ever seen. Starting with the separation of the spiritual from the temporal power, and the mutual independence of each in its own sphere, Catholicism worked hand in hand with feudalism for the amelioration of mankind. Under the influence of feudalism slavery became serfdom, and aggressive was modified into defensive war. Under the influence of Catholicism the monasteries preserved learning, and maintained the sense of the unity of Christendom. Under the combined influence of both, grew up the lovely ideal of chivalry, moulding generous instincts into gallant institutions,—making the body vigorous and the soul pure,—and wedding the Christian virtues of humility and tenderness to the natural graces of courtesy and strength. During this period the Church was the one mighty witness for light in an age of darkness, for order in an age of lawlessness, for personal holiness in an epoch of licentious rage. Amid the despotism of kings and the turbulence of aristocracies, it was an inestimable blessing that there should be a power which, by the unarmed majesty of simple goodness, made the haughtiest and the boldest respect the interests of justice, and tremble at the thought of temperance, righteousness, and the judgment to come.

i. But in the last three of these nine centuries, when the Church had achieved her destiny, the germs of new peril were insidiously developed. Faith and intellect began to be sundered, and violence was used for the repression of independent thought. The relations between the spiritual and temporal authorities were disturbed. Kings warred to the death with popes. Popes struggled to put their feet upon the necks of kings. The Avignonese captivity, followed as it was by the great schism of the papacy, shook to the ground the fabric so toilfully erected. Princes and nations successfully resisted a spiritual power which, by becoming ambitious, had become corrupt. Nations outgrew their spiritual nonage. The marks of that blow upon the cheek which William de Nogaret inflicted on Boniface the VIIIth were ineffaceable, and they typified the final rebellion of States against the political dominance of Churches,—the final liberation of thought and science from the shackles of ecclesiastical dogma,—the final victory of the Civil over the Canon law.

ii. Then came the revival of learning, and that epoch which we call the Renaissance. Never, perhaps, was the Faith of Christ in more terrible danger than in the 15th century. It was a state of society remarkably glittering and surpassingly corrupt—radiant with outward splendour, rotten with internal decay. Christendom had practically ceased to be Christian. Priests, turned atheists, made an open scoff of the religion they professed; scholars filled their writings with blasphemy and foulness[1]; a semi-heathen classicalism degraded even the

[1] To students of history the mere names of Della Casa, Folengo, Bandello, Filelfo, Bibbiena, Bembo, Pomponatus and Poggio are enough. Some of these men abused each other through folio pages of a scurrility wholly untranslatable—" quæ etiam prostituti ut meretricarii verentur verbis proferre." The disgusting *Facetiæ* of Poggio passed through twenty editions between 1470 and 1500. See K. v. Raumer, *Gesch. d. Pädagogik*, pp. 37—65, Burckhardt,

most sacred phrases into a sickening travesty of Pagan idioms[1]; the tenth Lateran Council found it necessary to repromulgate the doctrine of immortality[2]; and a

Die Kultur d. Renaissance in Italien, 1860. He shows that, as usual, corruption went hand in hand with the grossest superstition. "Il y avait à cette époque *une perversité raisonnée et scientifique*, une magnifique ostentation de scélératesse; disons tout d'un môt, le prêtre athée se croyait roi du monde." Michelet, *Mém. de Luther* I. 13. For other quotations, see Luthardt, *Apolog. Vorträge*, 244 (6te *Aufl.*) Aretino, an atheist, a libeller, a coward, a man of disgraceful immorality, and yet the friend of Titian, and the terror of Kings and Popes who flattered him, is the consummation of all that is worst in the epoch:

"Chi giace l'Aretin poeta tosco,
Che dice mal d'egnun fuor che di dio,
Sensandosi col dire, '*Non lo conosco.*'"

The pride, corruption, worldliness, hollowness, and greed of this age are often unveiled in the writings of Mr Ruskin, and are wonderfully pictured in Mr Browning's poem, "The Bishop Orders his Tomb in St. Praxed."

[1] Cardinal Bembo—he of the forty portfolios, through which he passed every sentence till it had attained the requisite amount of polish—talks of the Holy Spirit as "*aura Zephyri* Celestis" (*Epp. Leonis nomine Scripta*, III. 21); the Blessed Virgin as *Dea Ipsa* (Id. VIII. 17.); saints as *relati inter divos;* Christ as Minerva sprung from the head of Jupiter, and so on. Pulci writes in his *Morgante*.

"O giusto, O sante, O eterno Monarca,
O Sommo giove per noi crocifisso!"

Michelet, *Mém. de Luther*, I. 17, quotes many other instances. See too Bunsen, *Gott in der Geschichte*, V. 9. He quotes the remarkable testimony of Petrarch's *Sonnets*, CVI. CVII.

[2] In 1513 Bembo thought all the worse of Melanchthon because he believed in the immortality of the soul. Leo X. allowed the question to be discussed in his presence, and openly protected Pomponatius, whose work, *De Immortalitate Animæ*, seemed

Pope jested with his secretary on the profitableness to them of the fable of Christ[1]. All seemed to be lost and dead, when the voice of Luther's indignation shook the world. The strength of the Reformers lay not only in their intrinsic grasp of the truths which they set forth, but also in the corruption, the avarice, the infidelity which they exposed. The greed of Clement V., the haughtiness of Boniface VIII., the frantic violence of Urban VI., the unutterable degradation of John XXIII., the glittering insincerity of Leo X.,—these were what added the roll of vindictive thunder to Luther's words[2]. The heroic devotion of Ignatius Loyola came an age too late. The Romish hierarchy fell, but Christian truth was saved. Sacerdotalism was ruined for ever; but the paramount authority of Scripture, the indefeasible right of individual judgment, the duty and the dignity of progress, the ultimate sovereignty of the race over the in-

expressly designed to make the doctrines of Christianity ridiculous. Roscoe, *Leo X*. II. 248 (ed. Bohn); Bayle, *Dict.*, *Art.* Leo X. "Politianus *totam sacram lectionem aspernabatur.*" Lud. Vives.

[1] See Roscoe, *Leo X*. II. pp. 388, 1488. Roscoe inclines to disbelieve the story, but as Raumer says (*Gesch. der Pädagogik*, p. 59 sq.), there is no internal evidence of its improbability. In Milman's *Latin Christianity* the reader may see what kind of things not only John XXIII., but even such Popes as Boniface VIII. and Urban VI. are sworn to have said about Christianity.

[2] Such names as Alexander VI., Sixtus IV., Innocent VIII., Julius II., &c., might well be added to the rôle. "In the 15th and 16th centuries," says Mr Lecky, "the intellectual influences which had long been corroding the pillars of the Church had done their work, and a *fearful moral retrogression*, aggravated by the newly-acquired ecclesiastical wealth, accompanied the intellectual advance." *Hist. of Rationalism*, I. p. 61.

dividual, the national independence from all centralized spiritual authority, were established on bases which, so long as the world lasts, can never be removed[1]. The hollow majesty of an artificial unity was replaced by the vigour, freshness, and intensity of an individual faith.

But, once more, the pendulum oscillated too far, and individualism brought its own perils. Carrying to an extreme this revolt against authority, and license of personal judgment during the 17th century, Hobbes in England, Spinoza in Holland, Bayle in France, inaugurated the movement, which, in the 18th century, produced that *second* crisis of infidelity in which it seemed as though the Church must be lost for ever. And what was the issue? How did the world prosper without religion? What need to dwell on that age of "the trifling head, and the corrupted heart"? When, in the chambers of St Louis, a worse than Sardanapalus suffered adulteresses to toy with the crown of France; when a worse than Messalina befouled with lust and assassination the throne of Russia[3]; when in Saxony an

[1] "Of what avail are the pigmy hands stretched forth to arrest the progress of the human race? What can they accomplish?" De Lamennais.

[2] Roman Catholic writers constantly assert that Scepticism was the offspring of Protestantism. But was Voltaire a Protestant? or Bayle? or the Encyclopædists? or Comte? or Renan? or Littré, Ste Beuve, and so many of the French littérateurs? or again the French school of very advanced materialists?

[3] Catherine II.:
"That foul woman of the north,
The lustful murderess of her wedded lord."
Coleridge, *Rel. Musings*.

Augustus the Strong well-nigh equalled the infamies of a Commodus[1], and in Prussia a Frederic II. made his court the propaganda of anti-Christian thought, and in England—alas! even in England—an English archbishop complimented an English queen on her placid indifference to her husband's sins[2]; in a word, when effeminacy and blasphemy were the all-but-universal concomitants of an all-but-universal disbelief[3]; in *that* picture we see what the 18th century was, what the 15th had been, and—*quod Deus omen avertat*—what the 19th may become[4]. If literature be a fair test of a nation's

---

[1] A sketch of this disgraceful person may be found in Carlyle's *Frederic the Great.*

[2] Blackbourne, Archbishop of York, told Queen Caroline that he had been talking to her minister Walpole about the new mistress, "and was glad to find that Her Majesty was such a sensible woman as to like her husband should divert himself." Cave, in the Dedication of his *Primitive Christianity*, says, "I beheld religion generally laid waste, and Christianity *ready to draw its last breath*, stifled and oppressed with the vice and impietie of a debauched and profligate age."

[3] See a very clever book by L. F. Bungener, *Voltaire et son Temps: Études sur le Dixhuit. Siècle.* Lacordaire has described this epoch in one of his finest bursts of eloquence (*Conférences*, 1846), but chiefly with reference to France. For the state of England the reader may consult Massey, *Hist.* 11. pp. 38—44, 49—89, with the references, or Miss Wedgwood's *Life of Wesley;* for Germany, Carlyle's *Frederic the Great*, passim.

[4] Witness Mazzini's description of this age (*Works*, VI. p. 69). "Belief is extinct, there is only its pretence; prayer is no more, there is only a movement of the lips; true love is no more, desire has taken its place; the holy warfare of *ideas* is abandoned, the conflict is that of interests. The worship of great thoughts has passed away. That which *is* raises the tattered banner of some

condition, is there any literature—not excepting a few vile and recent specimens in England, America, and France—much more revolting than the foul poetry of the cinque-centisti, or the corrupt and enervating fiction that dates from Diderot and Voltaire? The very wit and genius of these men is like a jewel of gold in a swine's snout, or a diamond on the mouldering forehead of a skull. To pass from them to those who held the faith which, forsooth, they affected to despise,—to pass from a Politian and an Aretino to a Fénelon or a Melanchthon, from Voltaire to Bossuet, or from Tom Paine to Leighton—is like stepping from a dark charnel-house into a glorious cathedral, and from thence into the pure air of the sunny or starlit sky. And was the world better for thus throwing overboard its faith in Christ? did the world succeed when it had tried to get rid of Christianity? Ay, my brethren, if it be success to boast of liberty and end in a reign of terror; of humanity, and end in Robespierre; of virtue, and to end in the worship of a harlot on the polluted altars of Notre Dame [1].

corpse-like traditions; that which would be hoists only the standard of physical wants, of material appetites." Materialism is the real danger of this age; but when "theology has been converted into anthropology," which Feuerbach calls "the task of modern times" (*Grundsätze d. Philosophie d. Zukunft*, II. p. 269), then, there being no God left and no doctrine of Immortality, men " may continue illogically to utter the holy words *progress* and *duty, but they have deprived the first of its basis, and the second of its source.*" See much more very powerfully argued to the same effect in Mr Mazzini's paper, *Fortnightly Rev.*, June, 1870, pp. 727—730.

[1] " Culture without religious consciousness is nothing but

VII. But when this plague of irreligion was foulest throughout society, once more God took pity on an apostate civilization, and purged the pestilence from the reeking atmosphere with fire and storm. He awoke, and His enemies were scattered. The great earthquake-shock of the French Revolution shook the minds of men from their frivolous and atheistic dreams. The finger of God wrote His Mene and Tekel in flame upon the guilty palace-walls, and, when His judgments were abroad in the world, the children of men learnt wisdom.

Let us then take warning, for indeed in what we have seen there is warning both for the world and for the Church. For the world, because it shows what diseases are virulent when men prefer the vapours of the death-vault to the incense of the cathedral: for the Church, because, even from this rough survey, it is abundantly clear what makes her unassailable and what makes her weak. Wealth, luxury, ambition, worldliness, vice; these have wounded her well-nigh to death,

---

civilized barbarism and disguised animalism." Bunsen, *Gott in der Gesch.* VI. 5. No one has stated more clearly than Göthe—whose testimony will be unsuspected—that epochs of faith are epochs of fruitfulness; and that epochs of unbelief, however glittering, are barren of all permanent good. See *West-östliche Divan* (*Werke*, iv. 264). It may be interesting to some readers to know that the unfortunate "goddess of reason," who had been adored with bacchanalian dances, as she sat in white robes, blue mantle and red cap with a pike in her hand on the altar of Notre Dame, *died so late as Sep.* 30, 1863, ninety years old, idiotic, blind, and a beggar in Alsace. See Christlieb, *Moderne Zweifel am Christlichen Glauben*, s. 152.

when she has been invincible against the scimitar of Mohammedan or the violence of Hun. So far back as the complaints of Clemens and the denunciations of Chrysostom against the gorgeous iniquities of Alexandria and Constantinople[1], we hear the warning note of peril, and learn that "golden priests who used wooden chalices are stronger than priests of wood with chalices of gold." "You see that the day is past when the Church could say, 'Silver and gold have I none,'" said Innocent IV. complacently to St Thomas of Aquinum, as he pointed to the masses of treasure which were being carried into the Vatican. "Yes, holy father," was the saint's reply; "and the day is also past when she could say to the paralytic, 'Take up thy bed and walk.'" But from age to age God left not Himself without witness; and from age to age the most mighty apology for Christianity has been in the lives of her saints. These have averted from guilty nations the rain of fire. Other religions have withered into dishonoured decrepitude; but she, with continuous rejuvenescence, has renewed her strength like the eagle; has run and not been weary, has walked and not been faint. If ever, through her own faithlessness, she has fallen before her enemies, she has risen Antæus-like, with new vigour, "and shaken her invincible locks." How many of her witnesses have, in ages of corruption, exclaimed like the Maccabees of old, "Let us die in our integrity." And never, though she seemed to be dying, never in her worst days has she lacked "the viaticum of good examples."

[1] Clem. Alex. *Pædag.* II. Cap. iii. iv. §§ 35—44.

The tenth century was dark, yet it produced an Anselm and a Bernard; the 15th was corrupted, yet in it lived a Savonarola and a Huss; martyrs, hermits, monks; schoolmen, like St Bonaventura and St Thomas; kings, like Alfred and St Louis; noble ladies, like St Theresa and St Elizabeth of Hungary; bishops, like St Edmund of Canterbury and St Carlo Borromeo; dissenters, like Bunyan and Whitfield; country pastors, like Oberlin and Lavater; modern statesmen, like Wilberforce and Montalembert; modern clergymen, like Robertson and Lacordaire; these are her best defenders. The "*Nos soli innocentes*¹" has ever been her best appeal. The sword of her power may be beaten down, but what fiery dart shall pierce the silver shield of her innocence? *There*, my brethren, there is an Apology in which, to the grave, we may all take part; for that shield may be upheld by the weakest and meanest arm. It may not be ours to utter convincing arguments, but it may be ours to live holy lives. It may not be ours to be subtle and learned and logical, but it may be ours to be noble and sweet and pure. Oh! believe me, not to the diadem of Constantine, not to the tiara of Gregory, not to the gorgeousness of Leo, not to the faggots of Torquemada, not to the sword of the Crusaders, not to the logic of the schoolmen, does Chris-

---

¹ οὐκ ἐν λόγοις ἀλλ' ἐν ἔργοις τὰ τῆς ἡμετέρας θεοσεβείας πράγματα. Just. Mart. *Parænes. ad Græc.* p. 33; Athenagoras, *Legatio,* p. 11; Tert. *Apolog.* 45. "Ah! quel argument contre l'incrédule que la vie du Chrétien!...Non, l'homme n'est pas ainsi par lui-même; quelque chose de plus qu'humain règne ici!" Rousseau.

tianity owe one half-hour of her dominion over any human heart; but to the majesty of her self-denials, to the beauty of her holiness, to the meekness of her saints, to the truth, the zeal, the faithfulness of those who asked for nothing better than to follow His example who died as a malefactor to save the world. And these lessons are open to us no less than to them. "They ask me for *secrets* for attaining to perfection," said St Francis de Sales; "for my part I know no other secret than this: to love God with all one's heart, and one's neighbour as oneself[1]." This was the great lesson of Christianity, but Christianity was not only a doctrine but a Life. Oh, let us strive to imitate that Life; take it with you, my young brethren, into the dust and glare of the busy world; amid the struggles and duties of this place of learning now, amid the temptations of great cities and eager lives hereafter, into the country parsonage and the lawyer's chambers, the merchant's counting-house and the soldier's tent; take but this with you, and—pure, happy, noble, confident—you may smile hereafter when men tell you that Christianity is dead. Do this, and it shall never die; it shall grow younger with years; it shall deepen in faith and wisdom, in dominion and power, in purity and peace; the dew of its birth shall be as the womb of the morning[2], and all they who believe and live thereby shall shine as the brightness of the firmament, and as the stars for ever and ever[3].

[1] Maxims of St François de Sales.
[2] Psalm cx. 3.   [3] Dan. xii. 3.

IV.

CHRISTIANITY AND THE INDIVIDUAL.

'Εν αὐτῷ γὰρ ζῶμεν καὶ κινούμεθα καί ἐσμεν.—Acts xvii. 28.

1 Thess. V. 23.

And the very God of peace sanctify you wholly; and I pray God your whole spirit, and soul, and body be preserved blameless unto the coming of our Lord Jesus Christ.

THE reasonableness, the historic evidence, the victorious progress of our faith—these are the considerations which have occupied us hitherto. But the Witness of History to Christ would have been imperfect did it not also prove that this steady triumph was the greatest of all blessings to the world. It remains therefore, so far as our brief limits will allow, to show, by clear facts, the nature of that faith, its beneficence, its universality, its occupation of the entire realm of human intelligence, its satisfaction of man's deepest yearnings, its adaptation to his loftiest aims. To-day we shall be occupied mainly with its relations to the individual life; and we shall hope to show how infinitely Christ transcends all other teachers: how infinitely Christianity transcends all other truths.

The Cross conquered, as we have seen; but what did the doctrine of the Cross effect for those among whom it prevailed? My brethren, we know alas!—well, perhaps, could it be known no more—what was the condition of the civilized world when the true Light first dawned upon its darkness. We know its haughty power, its brilliant refinement, its unutterable shame. Arrayed like the Apocalyptic harlot in gems and purple, its heart was stony with cruelty and diseased with lust. Robed like the blaspheming Herod in tissue of silver, within it was eaten of worms [1]. Its literature—so elaborate, so sad, so stained—is a true reflex of its state. Would we see its emperors—priests, atheists, and gods?[2]—a Suetonius and a Seneca will point us to specimens of them in a Tiberius at Capri or a Nero at Puteoli [3]. Would we know its patricians?—we may read in the compressed and haughty page of Tacitus the intensity of their terror and the agony of their despair. Would we learn some-

---

[1] Compare the beautiful lines of Mr Matthew Arnold ‹

"On that hard Pagan world disgust
 And sated loathing fell;
Deep weariness and sated lust
 Make human life a hell.
In his cool hall with haggard eyes
 The Roman noble lay,
He drove abroad in furious guise
 Along the Appian way.
He made a feast, drank fierce and fast,
 And crowned his hair with flowers;
No easier, nor no quicker passed
 The impracticable hours."

See too the grand passage in Milton's *Par. Regained*, IV. 132 :

"That people, victor once, now vile and base,
 Deservedly made vassal," &c.

[2] "Les Romains étaient éclairés; cependant ces mêmes Romains ne furent pas choqués de voir réunir dans la personne de César, *un dieu, un prêtre, et un athée.*" Gibbon, *Miscell. Works*, IV. 61.

[3] Tac. *Ann.* IV. 67, and *passim*.

thing of its populace?—a Petronius and an Apuleius paint for us their sinful amusements, their gluttonous debaucheries, their sanguinary rage. And if we would fain believe that these atrocities of the circus, and pollutions of the theatre, were but the thick scum on the surface of a guilty capital,—that too would be an idle hope. It was not only the hills of Rome, or the double beach of Corinth, or the sweet grove of Daphne by Orontes that witnessed the degrading worship of Thammuz or Laverna, of Cotytto or Cybele: no, the same poison had infected each sweet rural village and seaside town; and he who has seen amid the ruins of Pompeii the fragments of the secret staircase, in the little Temple, up which the priests of Isis crept to ventriloquise behind the deceptive statue their lying oracles,—or those chambers of the Gynæceum glowing with the unclean imagery of a prostituted art,—he who has realized how, amid such surroundings, the *curse* of a Paganism which had lost all reverence for man's chastity or woman's honour, must have been imbreathed with the first lessons of consciousness even by innocent childhood [1],—he may almost wonder that it did not please God to rebaptise that

---

[1] How could it be otherwise in a little town where there were obscene symbols on well-nigh every wall, door, and vessel; and where the odiously-degraded inscriptions betray what a German writer well calls "*dieser ganze grässliche heidnische Quark von Sodom und Gomorrha.*" The Museo Borbonico at Naples contains the most hideous visible proofs of the abject infamy of a dying Paganism. The common Pompeian inscriptions show an abysmal degradation which could not have been exceeded even by the Cities of the Plain.

world in another flood, which should have submerged for ever the dead traces of its turpitude,—or at least to calcine under the fiery lava the memorials of a degradation which might have made the very marble blush. It is an awful thing—this preservation of a witness against themselves by those who have long mingled with the common dust—this exhumation of forgotten iniquities and unveiling of their most secret receptacles into the cold revealing glare of day. But think not that it was for no purpose that the Erinnys of the dawn has been thus suffered to avenge the crimes of night. No: God willed that we should see by palpable proofs how, amid all its boasted wisdom, the heart of the heathen world was darkened into foolishness[1], and that the condition which some would gloss over with the name of a healthy animalism was in reality a sick and sickening putrescence. But it is dangerous to gaze even for a moment down the abysses into which the nature of man may fall; nor ought we even for purposes of instruction[2] to forget the true and manly lesson which a heathen has taught us —*Scelera ostendi oportet dum puniuntur: abscondi fla-*

[1] ἐματαιώθησαν ἐν τοῖς διαλογισμοῖς αὐτῶν καὶ ἐσκοτίσθη ἡ ἀσύνετος αὐτῶν καρδία. φάσκοντες εἶναι σοφοὶ ἐμωράνθησαν. Rom. i. 21, 22.

[2] "Many accounts there are in history scandalous...even unto humanity, *and whose not only verities but relations honest men do deprecate. We desire no record of such enormities;* in things of this nature silence commendeth History." Sir Thos. Browne, *Vulgar Errors*. I cannot forbear adding that I do not think Christian teachers have been by any means sufficiently careful to keep this fact in mind.

gitia[1]. For us, let it have been enough to glance with a shudder, and to pass by not unwarned; let it be enough to note how, in his Epistle to the Romans, the great Apostle who was its contemporary seized, as it were, that haughty, glittering, abominable civilization, and with firm hand, in letters which are indelible, branded upon its insolent and shameless brow the festering stigma of his stern and terrible rebuke[2].

Such then was the world into which—not to destroy but to revivify,—not to annihilate but to ennoble,—the Apostles of Christ passed forth to preach His doctrine.

---

[1] Tac. *Germ.* 12. "We can but stand at the cavern's mouth and cast a single ray of light into its dark depths. Were we to enter, our lamp would be quenched by the foul things which would cluster round it," *Seekers after God*, p. 38, where I have endeavoured to give a slight sketch of the state of Roman society at this period. One sentence from Seneca will be enough: "Omnia sceleribus et vitiis plena sunt . . . certatur ingenti quodam nequitiæ certamine . . . nec furtiva jam scelera sunt; præter oculos eunt. Adeoque in publicum missa nequitia est, et in omnium pectoribus evaluit, *ut innocentia non rara sed nulla sit.*" *De Ira*, II. 8; cf. Juv. *Sat.* XIII. 26—30; Marc. Aurel. *Commnet.* passim.

[2] Rom. i. 21—32. All that can be said on heathen morality —(and far too much has been said on many phases of it, of which it would have been better to say with Dante (*Inferno*, III. 51),

"Non ragioniam di lor, ma guarda e passa")—

is but a commentary on this awful paragraph. Notice the play of words, almost untranslatable in English, in v. 28. "And as they did not *choose* (or reprobated) to keep God in their knowledge, God gave them over to a mind *that could not choose* (or reprobate), so that they did things not convenient." The paronomasia turns on the double meaning of δοκιμάζω, and it implies, as a recent commentator has remarked, "*a retributive justice in kind, beginning even in this life.*"

Silently, insensibly, but with certain transformation, like the leaven in the meal, that doctrine made its way. We have seen how the heathens emptied upon it the vials of their fury and their scorn; how Rabbi and Sophist, Pontifex and Emperor joined hand in hand for its destruction; and yet, long before Christians were known as anything but a strange sect, who could stand in the fire without a tremor, and face the Libyan tiger with a smile,—long before they had won the shadow of a material victory,— the truths which they taught had largely moulded the opinions of their persecutors. We catch the echo of them in a Seneca, we listen to their very accents in an Aurelius. The vernal breeze of this new religion breathed health and hope into a decrepit Paganism for many a long year before the spring itself had dawned; the morning was spread upon the mountains for two centuries before its glory reached the plains.

It is not—and to this point I would ask attention— it is not that we claim a mere antecedence and originality for the separate precepts of Christianity. Their victory, their beneficence, their unique superiority were not due to this. Many of those precepts, viewed as mere literary utterances, had been enounced in the world before. No small portion even of the Lord's prayer may be found, it is believed, in Hebrew writings[1]. To us there is absolutely no point in the sneer of sceptics[2],

[1] See Ecclus. xxviii. 1—9, &c.; Grotius, *De Verit. Relig. Christ.* I. 10, &c., *ad Matt.* vi. 9.

[2] To the foolish attempts to attribute these to plagiarism, and to the curious combinations to which it has given rise, I have alluded elsewhere. See *Seekers after God*, pp. 181, 182, 320. To the

that the most distinctive rules of Christianity may be paralleled from secular sources. On the contrary, we have always rejoiced to know that God left not Himself without witness, and that what St Paul so finely describes as His richly-variegated wisdom, had long been visible in part by that light which lighteth every man that is born into the world [1]. It is perfectly true that, if from east to

instances there given, may be added the attempt to insinuate that Philo, in his old age, had seen some of the Apostles during his visit to Rome and borrowed from them. The idleness of such charges may be measured by the countercharge of Celsus, that Christianity had plagiarized from the philosophers. Almost the whole of the VIth book of Origen against Celsus is devoted to a refutation of this charge. Christian Wolff was actually expelled from his Chair at Halle by the King of Prussia, and forbidden to return "under penalty of death," for an eulogy on the ethical teachings of Confucius! Hagenbach, *Germ. Ration.* (E. tr.) p. 35. "I must consider it wrong and robbery in you," wrote Göthe playfully to Lavater, "to pluck all the various feathers of the beautiful birds under heaven and adorn your bird of Paradise exclusively with them." The great Greek fathers took a far nobler line (see next note). On the other hand, we should be perfectly open to receive evidence, where it actually exists, of the direct action of Christianity on philosophies and religions. It is, for instance, by no means impossible that the legend of Krishna may have been in part developed out of confused reminiscences of Gnostic writings. The Gospel of the Infancy was very popular in the East. Lassen admits a *possibility* of Christian influence on the Puránas. See Wilson, *Hindu Sects*, and R. Williams, *Christianity and Hinduism*, p. 295. For the possibility of such influence on Chinese Buddhism, see *Travels of Fah Hian* (tr. Beal), lxxii., lxxiii. Many of the Jewish books, again, are now thought to belong to *a very much later date* than was originally believed.

[1] "Taceo de Philosophis quos...nonnullus etiam afflatus veritatis adversus Deos erigit." Tert. *Ad. Nat.* I. 10. "Encore que les Philosophes soient les protecteurs de l'erreur," says Bossuet,

west we ransack the literature and the philosophy of the habitable globe, we may here and there cull some memorable aphorism resembling those which *we* too reverence in our heritage of moral truths; and, at epochs separated from each other by thousands of years, it is possible to catch now and then a glimpse of those prismatic hues which may be combined into the pure white ray of Christian doctrine. Not only in the writings of the later Stoicism, when already through the despairing twilight a luminous haze had been diffused[1],—not only

"toutefois ils ont *frappé à la porte de la vérité.* (Veritatis fores pulsant, Tert.) S'ils ne sont pas entrés dans son sanctuaire, s'ils n'ont pas eu le bonheur de le voir et de l'adorer dans son temple, ils se sent quelquefois présentés à ses portiques, et lui ont rendu de loin quelque homage." *Panég. de Ste Cathérine.* On this subject, however, the Latin Fathers are rhetorical, and confused, and insincere; *e.g.*, we find Tertullian in other places positively coarse in his attacks on the philosophers (*Apol.* 46), &c.; on one page we find Minuc. Felix contemptuously calling Socrates "*Scurra Atticus*," *Oct.* 38, while a little before he says: "Ut quivis arbitretur aut nunc Christianos philosophos esse, *aut philosophos fuisse jam Christianos.*" *Id.* 20. On the other hand, while such writers as Tatian and Athenagoras take the violent and unjustifiable line— Tatian descending to such an abyss of absurdity as to say that the Greek language itself is one great plagiarism (ὥσπερ ὁ κολοιὸς οὐκ ἰδίοις ἐπικοσμούμενος πτεροῖς!)—the great Alexandrian Fathers, Justin Martyr, Origen and Clement, write in the noblest and most charitable spirit, *e.g.*, ἃ μὲν κινούμενοι εἰρήκασιν, Clem. Alex. *Strom.* VI. 7, § 55. οἱ πάντες τὰ ἡμέτερα μιμούμενοι λέγουσι, Just. Mart. *Apol.* I. 51, II. 93. Ὁ θεὸς μὲν αὐτοῖς ταῦτα καὶ ὅσα καλῶς λέλεκται ἐφανέρωσεν, Orig. *c. Cels.* VI. 9, VII. 28—30.

[1] τῆς Χριστιανικῆς θεολογίας πολλὰ τοῖς οἰκείοις ἀνέμιξαν λόγοις. Theodor. *de Cur. Græc. affect.* II. We believe this to be to a great extent true of the later Stoics, although in all probability they were themselves wholly unconscious of the fact, and would have

AND THE INDIVIDUAL. 137

In the open plagiarisms of the *Koran*, spoiled so often in the plagiarising,—but, even centuries before Christ, in the Dialogues of Socrates, in the Republic of Plato, in the Analects of Confucius, in the Laws of Manou, in the Sútras of the Buddhists, in the Vedas of the Brahmins, in the Zend Avesta of the Parsis, in the Pirke Avoth[1] of the Rabbis, there are unquestionably precepts which might be combined into a very pure and noble code[2].

indignantly denied it. But we do not say this because we value these truths "as the miser values his pearls and precious stones, thinking their value lessened if pearls and precious stones of the same kind are found in other parts of the world." Max Müller, *Chips*, I. That the Neoplatonists borrowed from Christianity is clear, though they misunderstood its very essence. Some have believed that Ammonius Saccas, the founder of Neolatonism, was an apostate Christian.

[1] Specimens may be found in Otho, *Lex. Rabb.* pp. 39, 163, 410, sq.

[2] The two following passages will express the truest aspect of this matter. Τὸν Χριστὸν τοῦ Θεοῦ πρωτότοκον εἶναι ἐδιδάχθημεν, καὶ προεμηνύσαμεν ὡς Λόγον ὄντα οὗ πᾶν γένος ἀνθρώπων μέτεσχε καὶ οἱ μετὰ Λόγου βιώσαντες Χριστιανοί εἰσι κἂν ἄθεοι ἐνομίσθησαν, ὡς ἐν"Ελλησι μὲν Σωκράτης καὶ 'Ηρακλεῖτος καὶ οἱ ὅμοιοι αὐτοῖς...οἱ δὲ μετὰ Λόγου βιώσαντες καὶ βιοῦντες Χριστιανοὶ καὶ ἄφοβοι καὶ ἀτάραχοι ὑπάρχουσιν. Just. Mart. *Apol.* I. 46. 'Ήδη δὲ καὶ καθολικῷ λόγῳ πάντα ἀναγκαῖα καὶ λυσιτελῆ τῷ βίῳ θεόθεν ἥκειν εἰς ἡμᾶς λέγοντες οὐκ ἂν ἁμάρτοιμεν, τὴν δὲ φιλοσοφίαν καὶ μᾶλλον "Ελλησιν οἷον διαθήκην οἰκείαν αὐτοῖς δεδόσθαι ὑποβάθραν οὖσαν τῆς κατὰ Χριστὸν φιλοσοφίας. Clem. Alex. *Strom.* VI. 8. § 67 (and *passim*). See Jam. i. 17. The passages in which the heathen writers approved the truths of Christian morality have often been collected. See Ackermann, *Das Christliche in Plato*, Hamburg, 1835; Schneider, *Christliche Klänge aus dem Griech. und Röm. Classik.* 1865; Martha, *Les Moralistes Romains;* Aubertin, *Sénèque et St Paul*, &c.

Yet what candid reasoner, even were he an unbeliever in Christianity, could dream of comparing any one of these sacred books, or the men who originated them, or the systems in which they issued, with the Gospels, or with Christianity, or with Christ? With every desire to admit their services, with no temptation to depreciate their worth, what is the calm and deliberate judgment which History forces us to pronounce? Confucius was a sage, yet he correctly described himself as "a transmitter, not a maker;" his example, in more than one respect, was distinctly questionable; he reduced religion to a reflexive ceremony of empty proprieties; he gave no impulse to holiness; he had no sympathy with progress; and to him, beyond all question, in the opinion of close and candid witnesses, is due, in great measure, the falsity, the senility, the atrophy, moral and intellectual, of the vast race which chose him as their ideal[1]. The Buddha Sakya Mouni, so far as we can disentangle his real life from a mass of monstrous and often senseless traditions[2], is one of the noblest and purest figures in History; yet there was a needless and uncleanly abjectness in several of his precepts; his religion is a blank and dreary atheism; his morality a narrow selfishness; his heaven an extinction of sentient existence; his loftiest social action a perverted bodily service[3]. Mohammed, though we may smile at the ignorant bigotry which in

---

[1] See Appendix B, Confucius.
[2] Some have even questioned his real existence, but this seems to be an excess of scepticism. See Wilson, *Hindu Sects*.
[3] See Appendix C, Buddha.

the Middle Ages made his name synonymous with that of Satan, yet not only by the authentic voice of tradition, but also in his own book[1], stands self-condemned of immoderate passions and wavering will, and the modified Judaism which he attempted to revivify[2] has proved to be a fatal legacy to most of the nations who have adopted it. And what shall we say of Socrates and Plato? There have been many who have ventured to place Socrates by the side of Christ;—and Socrates was great, and noble, and wise, and his death is one of the most moving scenes of ancient history; let us not breathe one word against that holy and high-souled sage,—but the truth is dearer to us even than Socrates; and when we think of Socrates conversing with Theodota[3], or feasting with Agathon[4],—when we remember the mingled leniency and coarseness with which he spoke of the sins of Critias,—when we recall his cold and almost impatient dismissal of his wife and children at his hour of approaching death[5], and then, with bowed head, think

[1] *e.g.*, His conduct towards the wife of Zaid, *Koran*, XXXIII. 36 (Rodwell's *Koran*, p. 567), and his Paradise with its flowing winecups that cause no headache, and its Houris with large dark eyes like pearls hidden in their shells. *Koran*, Sura LVI. 22 (Rodwell, p. 61).

[2] See Dr Deutsch on 'Islam,' in the *Quarterly Review;* Lane's *Modern Egyptians;* Palgrave's *Arabia;* and any modern book of travels in countries under the Turkish rule bears out this assertion. The success of Mohammedanism, such as it was, was due in no small measure to the lower tone it took,—to its almost cynical spirit of accommodation to the infirmities of nature. Imagine St Paul to have written such paragraphs as those quoted in the last note!

[3] Xen. *Mem.* II. II.   [4] Plato, *Symposium*, § 4.

[5] Plato, *Phæd.* § 9, ἀπαγαγέτω τις ταύτην οἴκαδε.

of Him who talked by the well-side with the woman of
Samaria, or stood alone by that guilty adulteress as she
sobbed upon the Temple floor,—or who, as He hung
upon the Cross between the thieves, chose out the ten
derest-hearted of His disciples, and, in the midst of His
anguish, said to His mother, "*Woman, behold thy son,*"—
then, indeed, if our spiritual sense be not utterly blunt
and dead, we may see how infinite is the gulf which
separates the teacher of Athens from the Son of God [1].
And Plato—the "*divinus ille Plato*" of Arnobius—the
Plato of whom Clement said that he touched the very
gates of truth [2]—the Plato whom Jerome carried with
him under his hermit mantle, and Augustine under his
bishop's [3] robe—the Plato whom our own Coleridge
called "A plank from the wreck of Paradise, cast upon
the shores of idolatrous Greece"—we all know the
depth of his insight, the subtlety of his reasoning, the
splendour of his imagination, the magic of his style; and

[1] It is needless to point out that in the Greek γύναι there is none
of the bluntness of the English "woman;" it was an address perfectly tender and courteous to the highest and best beloved. "Quels
préjugés, quel aveuglement ne faut-il point avoir pour oser com-
parer le fils de Sophronisque au fils de Marie! Quelle distance
de l'un à l'autre!" Rousseau, *Emile*, II. p. 110. See Rougemont,
Socrate et Jésus Christ. Neander, *Wissenschaftl. Abhandl.* (ed. Jacobi,
1851, p. 140, sqq).

[2] Ackermann, *Das Christliche in Plato*, 8.

[3] Augustine goes so far as to say that he could have pardoned
the pagans if, instead of raising a temple to Cybele, they had reared
a shrine in which the books of Plato should be read. *De Civ. Dei*,
ad fin. Numenius asked τί γάρ ἐστι Πλάτων ἢ Μωϋσῆς 'Αττικίζων;
Theodoret, *De Cur. Græc. affect*. II. p. 37; *Sylb*. Plato qui *omnium
sapientissimus* judicatur; Lactant. *Div. Inst.* I. 5, 23.

yet, when we think how overwhelming would have been the *shock* to our moral sense, how *fatal* the overthrow of our distinctions between right and wrong, had he been accepted as the world's teacher; when we place the *Phædrus* or the *Symposium* with all their poetic eloquence and all the subtly dangerous poison of their perfumed but unwholesome air, beside the sweet, pure, simple books of humble fishermen of Galilee;—when we compare his ideal republic with its community of women, its destruction of the family, its degradation of the multitude, its exposition of children, its tolerated, and worse than tolerated, crimes [1], with the Kingdom of Heaven as preached by Christ,—then must we not see in such a comparison, unless made by way of contrast, I will not say a gross injustice, but I will say—for so it is—an unwarrantable blasphemy against the simple truth. Ay, my brethren, the most golden idol of Pagan excellence stands but on feet of clay. There is flagrant intellectual error in their very wisest; there is fearful moral aberration in their very best. Over their graves, as in the sigh of the wailing wind, we hear the words, "*The world by wisdom knew not God*[2]." They were the foremost men of all ages in brilliant Greece, in stately Rome, in immemorial China, in imperial Persia, in free Arabia, in solemn Hindostan: the Buddha was a prince, wealthy, and beautiful, and strong; and Confucius was a descendant

[1] *De Rep.* v. 14, *Charmides*, x. Xen. *Mem.* I. 3. 14; VI. 14. Athen. v. p. 187. Döllinger, *The Gentile and the Jew* (tr. Oxenham), I. 357, II. p. 238, sqq. Zeller, *Philos. d. Griechen*, II. 569, and a chapter in Grote's *Plato*.

[2] 1 Cor. i. 21.

of nobles and a counsellor of kings; and Plato, with his haughty aristocratic genius, so towered over the greatest of his time, that they could only reach to lay their garlands of admiration at his feet;—yet to compare any one of these with Him who spent all but three years of His humble life as the carpenter of Nazareth[1], is to match a dim and uncertain twilight with the sun at noon; and the least in the Kingdom of Heaven—the least who obeys and loves his Lord—the most unlettered, the most ignorant, the most obscure—not perhaps in man's judgment, but in the judgment of the Angels and of God—the least in the Kingdom of Heaven is greater than these.

And why? not only because there was in the precepts of Christianity a reality, which, as precepts, they had never possessed before, not only because they rang more true, but also because *they* alone were active, living, efficacious, self-renewing[2]. The very best

[1] οὐχ οὗτός ἐστιν ὁ τέκτων; Mark vi. 3. That one word is almost the *only* ray of light shed on the personal history of our Lord's life during its first 30 years.

[2] An Ovid, no less than a St Paul, had felt the struggle between an intellect which *knew what was right* and a life that *practised what was wrong;* but Christianity alone revealed the secret which would heal the moral impulses of a perverted will. It would be easy to parallel Rom. vii. 14—24 from many pagan sources: but the next verse (25) and the whole of Rom. viii. remain *unique* and unapproachable by the loftiest exponents of heathen wisdom. See this argument powerfully stated by Tertullian, *Apolog.* 46; Lactant. *Div. Inst.* III. 26. Perhaps I may venture to quote one passage from a chapter which I have elsewhere devoted to the subject. " The morality of Paganism was, on its own confession, insufficient. It was tentative where Christianity is authoritative; it was dim and partial where Christianity is bright and complete; it was inadequate

systems of human philosophy were stricken with a fatal impotence. Like the gathered blossoms stuck in the careless garden of a child, they may look lovely for a time, but because they have no root they wither away. Ending mostly in high-sounding conversations among an illuminated few, they were powerless amid the general degradation either to awaken the conscience or to guide the life. Even when the truths of Christianity had insensibly pervaded the moral atmosphere, and the books and the lives which it inspired were in the hands and before the eyes of men, the very best and greatest of the heathen not only failed to surpass, but failed even at an immeasurable distance to rival them. Barely could they cast out the devil from their own souls[1]: they never aspired, in their hopelessness, to exorcise it from the society which it tormented. There is an eloquent wisdom and subtle charm in the writings of the Neronian minister, the crippled slave, the blameless Emperor; but in the Gospels and the Epistles

---

to rouse the sluggish carelessness of mankind where Christianity came with an imperial and awakening power; it gives only a rule where Christianity supplies a principle; and even where its teachings were absolutely identical with those of Scripture, it failed to ratify them with a sufficient sanction; it failed to announce them with the same powerful and contagious ardour; it failed to furnish an absolutely faultless and vivid example of their practice; it failed to inspire them with an irresistible motive; it failed to support them with a powerful comfort under the difficulties which were sure to be encountered in the aim after a consistent and holy life." *Seekers after God*, p. 319.

[1] "Nemo per se satis valet ut emergat, oportet manum aliquis porrigat, aliquis educat." Sen. *Ep.* 52.

we find no deep drawback, like the haughty apathy of the one, the concentrated egotism of the second, the unbroken sadness of the third[1]. And we too, in this century, have seen the attempted outline of a new religion. The philosopher who founded it was a man of singular goodness and varied erudition. The records of every belief, the truths of every philosophy, the discoveries of every science, the memorials of every life, the moral treasury of every land and age were at his disposal. He sketched a system which has won for him the adherence of eminent thinkers, and the love of many who glory "in the wide thought and the vast hope[2]." Some of those followers are known and honoured by many among us, and yet after careful study of this religion it seems to me incontestable that its wisest precepts are not original, and its most original are not wise. Its motto, " Live for others," is a grand motto, but is "altruism" a sweeter or better word than charity[3]? or, has the bare and naked formula, " *Vivre pour autrui*"

[1] There was a deep tone of pride, sadness, and egotism *throughout* all the later systems of philosophy. *Tota flebilis vita est*, Sen. *De Const. ad Marc.* x. 5. Cf. Herod. vii. 46. Marc. Aurel. *Epict.* But Minucius Felix says, "Christianus miser *videri potest, inveniri non potest.*" *Oct.* 37. On this subject see Dean Merivale's *Conversion of the Empire*, Lect. v.

[2] See Appendix D, Comte.

[3] Comte was a devoted admirer of the *Imitatio Christi*, which he daily studied, and which he recommended all his followers to study, substituting only Humanity for God ! He does not pretend that his motto was original. "I sum up," he says, "all my wishes for personal perfection in the admirable form by which the sublimest of mystics was led to prepare, in his own manner, the moral motto of Positivism, *Amem te plus quam me, nec me nisi propter te.*"

a charm which has been lost from the old commandment, " *Thou shalt love thy neighbour as thyself*[1] "? And by putting this forth, "not as the second Commandment," but as " the first to which there is no second[2]," the religion of Positivism degrades it from a living principle to an oratorical precept. For, dissevered from belief in God, such a precept is inoperative; dissociated from faith and prayer, it is impossible. And what, in fact, does Positivism offer us for the truths which it would sweep ruthlessly away? For Immortality, the impersonal absorption in a collective idea; for Prayer, the hollow sham of an imaginary petition poured into a non-existent ear,[3] : for the Father, the Son, and the Holy Spirit—*O cæcas hominum mentes !*—a new Trinity

Catech. of Pos. Rel. One of the Comtist mottoes is, "*Diis extinctis, Deoque, successit Humanitas.*"

[1] Precepts not wholly dissimilar may be found in heathen writers, *e.g.*, Hes. *Opp.* 1. 284, 303, 312; and in Confucius, *Chung Yung* (*Doctrine of the Mean*, ch. XX.); and still better in the Analects, when Tze Kung asks if there be one word which may serve as a rule of practice for all one's life, and is answered, " Is not reciprocity (*altruism*) such a word? *What you do not want done to yourself, do not do to others.*" *Anal.* XV. 23 in Legge's Confucius. In *Anal.* V. 11, he tells Tze that he has not attained to this. So too, to return good for evil, or something like it, may be found in the Laws of Manou (see Michelet, *Bible de l'Humanité*, p. 437). For Buddha's moral precepts, see Barth. St Hilaire, *Le Bouddha*, pp. 92—119. Yet unquestionably Confucianism and Buddhism are, in their social influence, gigantic failures; and in these cases, M. Renan says, "Success is a decisive criterion." Mr Mozley has forcibly pointed out that the heathen world failed not in *knowledge* but in *action*. *Bampt. Lect.* p. 171—173.

[2] Dr Bridges, *Unity of Comte's Life and Doctrine*, p. 5.

[3] " We adore her (Humanity)...in order to serve her better by

consisting of Humanity, the World and Space[1]! And oh, my brethren, is this all, which, after 3000 years of disputation, the latest Philosophy can offer as its substitute for a religion which makes man at peace with the world, at peace with his own conscience,' at peace with God; which offers a Redeemer to the sinful, a Saviour to the suffering, a Deliverer to the enslaved; which inspires life with the present sense of Eternity and the future hope of Heaven; which opens to guilt and peril the vision of safety, to despair and suffering the gates of hope[2]?

bettering ourselves;" thus prayer is for the Positivist "a work of art." Comte, *Cat. of Pos. Rel.* p. 106 sqq.

[1] "Thus we complete the Trinity of our Religion—Humanity, the World, and Space." Dr Congreve, *The New Religion in its Attitude to the Old*, p. 18. The same idea is repeated in the following passage: "We recall with gratitude the services which have hitherto been only unconsciously received from her coeval institution, SPACE—services of which we now unconsciously avail ourselves.... We commemorate the services of our common mother the EARTH, the planet on which we dwell....We commemorate the services of HUMANITY, the great organism of which we are inseparable parts." Id. *The Propagation of the New Religion.* One of the mottoes of Positivism is, *Reorganiser sans Dieu ni roi.* "Vous pretendez que tout va mal parceque Dieu n'est pas assez parmi nous; tandis que nous affirmons que tout irait bien mieux s'il n'y était pas du tout." De Sémérie, *Posit. et Catholiques*, p. 5.

[2] See Guizot, *Méditations sur l'Essence de la Rel. Chrétienne*, pp. 65—67, one of the most remarkable passages in a book well worth studying. Speaking of Confucius, Buddha, &c., he says " Ont ils réellement changé l'état moral et social des peuples? Ont ils imprimé à l'humanité un grand progrès et ouvert devant elle des horizons qu'avant eux elle ne courait pas? *Nullement*...En dehors du christianisme il y a eu de grands spectacles d'action et de force, de brillants phénomènes de génie et de vertu, de généreux essais de

Since then such is the superiority of Christianity, since it comes before us not as a mere collection of dogmas, or series of aphorisms, but as a living faith able to bridge over the broad gulf between knowledge and action, between our ideal and our life; we hardly care to waste time in proving its originality. It is indeed incontrovertibly original, in that it united what others had isolated; it concentrated what others had scattered; it harmonised what others had opposed; and, more than this, were it our object to maintain the claim, its mere vocabulary establishes its entire and noble independence. Where were the Greek or Latin words for "charity" till Christianity created them, and stamped them with her own divine image, and made them current amid the coins of a debased mintage, like pure and solid gold? Ἔρως, indeed, and *Amor* were words which Greek and Latin *did* possess, but they so reeked with heathen associations that Christianity could not rescue them from the mire in which they lay; but ἀγαπή[1] and *Caritas* with all the mighty revolution which they have effected, and all the angelic utterances which they have inspired, are the glory of Christianity

réforme, de savants systèmes philosophiques, et de beaux poëmes mythologiques; point de vraie, profonde, et féconde régénération de l'humanité et de la société."

[1] "'Ἀγαπή tota Christianorum est," ἔρως, ἐρᾶν, ἐραστής, unknown, to the N.T. See Archbp. Trench (*N. T. Synonyms, First series, s.v.*); and, on the other hand, if the reader will look out ἀγαπή in Liddell and Scott's Lexicon, he will merely see 'Ἀγαπή, 'brotherly love,' *Eccl.;* showing, that for classical purposes, the word had no existence. The Latin word *caritas* is indeed perfectly classical, but is connected with a wholly different range of conceptions from 'charity,'

alone. Or take *Humilitas*[1]; to the Christian it was one of the sweetest and saintliest of virtues, to the heathen one of the most pusillanimous of faults. Or again, take *Humanitas;* previous to the spread of Christianity it means chiefly human nature, or refined culture[2]; it is Christianity alone which breathed into it all that it connotes, and made it mean love to the whole brotherhood of man, united to the Universe by natural laws, united to God by the common mysteries of Creation and Redemption; united to all the dead by the continuity, to all the living by the solidarity of life. We do not concede, then, that Christianity is unoriginal even as a moral system[3]; and we besides maintain that no faith has ever been able, like it, to sway the affections and hearts of men. Other religions are defective and erroneous, ours is perfect and entire; their systems were esoteric, ours is universal[4]; theirs temporary and for the few, ours

---

[1] The classical *humilitas* is a term of strong contempt, '*abjectness*,' *e.g.*, "Malorum turba quædam paupertas, ignobilitas, *humilitas*," &c. Cic. *Tusc. Disp.* v. 10, cf. III. 13. A Greek would have been amazed to find ταπεινοφροσύνη reckoned among the virtues;—yet St Peter bids Christians *tie it on themselves like a knotted robe* (ἐγκομβώσατθε) 1 Pet. v. 5.

[2] Being mainly equivalent to the two Greek words, φιλανθρωπία and παιδεία. V. Forcellini, *s.v.*

[3] See on this subject some excellent remarks of Renan. He says, with perfect candour and justice, that in spite of all real and supposed parallels, "Il y a dans la doctrine du Christ *un esprit nouveaux et un cachet original.*" *Ét. d'Hist. Rel.* 188. "What the soul is to the body," says the author of the beautiful and striking *Epistle to Diognetus*, "that Christianity is to the world."

[4] Origen nobly reproaches Philosophy with its *exclusiveness*, and pretended monopoly of truth—(οὗτοι τὸ κοινωνικὸν εἰς κυμιὸν

eternal and for the race; a handful read the philosophers, myriads would die for Christ[1]; they in their popularity could barely found a school, Christ from His Cross rules the world; they could not even conceive the ideas of a society without falling into miserable error; Christ established an eternal and glorious Kingdom, whose theory for all, whose history in the world, prove it to be indeed what it was from the first proclaimed to be—the kingdom of Heaven, the kingdom of God.

Since then, my brethren, the individual virtues are the only true and solid bases of moral perfection, since they offer the most natural and decisive exercise for the ascendency of reason over the passions, let us devote the short remainder of our time this morning to testing the truth of what we have advanced, by comparing the doctrines of Christianity with other systems, in their influence upon the individual life; nor can we do this more briefly or decisively than by considering the nature and effect of the truths which it enforces in their relation to the Body, the Intellect, and the Soul of man.

1. On the exquisite workmanship of this tabernacle not made with hands, on the delicate and subtle

στενὸν καὶ βραχὺ συνήγαγον, c. Cels. VI. 1); and with its arrogance—(οὐδὲ τὸ 'Εμοὶ προσέχετε κἂν διδάσκωμέν φαμεν, c. Cels. v. 76).

[1] "Quotusquisque nunc Aristotelem legit? Quanti Platonis vel libros novere, vel nomen? vix in angustiis otiosi eos senes recolunt. Rusticanos vero et piscatores nostros totus orbis loquitur, universus mundus sonat." Jerome, ad Ep. ad Gal. iii. 3. "Let the human mind be expanded as much as it please," said Göthe, in one of his last conversations with Eckermann, "it will never transcend the height and morality of Christianity as it shines in the Gospel."

harmonies of this harp of a thousand strings, the Scriptures say but little[1]. For that task Science is abundantly competent; and, for the still loftier task of confirming by decisive evidence those solemn warnings of Holy Writ that men must possess in manhood the sins even of their youth[2]; that if they sow to the flesh they shall of the flesh reap corruption[3]; that the punishment of sensuality, working not by special interventions but by general laws, bears a fearful resemblance to the sin itself[4]; that the Nemesis of a desecrated body is an enfeebled understanding and a tormented and darkened soul. Much of this the heathen saw; and yet, even in a doctrine so simple and elementary as the relation of man to his own body, how egregiously even their best teachers went astray! On the one hand, to adore and pamper it, to treat it as all in all, to devote the whole life with frantic eagerness to the gratification of its evanescent pleasures or the flattery of its carnal pride[5]; on the other, to despise and villify it as the clog, and chain, and prison of the soul[6], and so to master and crush it with with hideous mutilations and ex-

[1] See, however, Ps. cxviii. 14, Eccl. xi. 5.
[2] Job xiii. 26, xx. 11.
[3] Gal. vi. 8.
[4] See the remarkable chapter in Wisdom of Solom. xi.
[5] 1 Cor. xv. 32.
[6] Plato, *Phæd.* xxiv. § 16; Virg. *Æn.* vi. 733; Cic. *Tusc. Disp.* i. 30; Sen. *Ep.* 65. "Corpus hoc animi *pondus ac pœna est.*" See Brucker, *Hist. Phil.* i. 1222, "Corpus contemnendum et stercore vilius judicandum." Similar was the mistake of Buddhism—to regard the body as an enemy to be subjugated, not as a friend to be ennobled. B. St Hilaire, *Le Bouddha*, p. 146.

extravagant self-torture,—these were the counter-errors of heathen philosophy and heathen life; these were the ethics of corporal duties as taught by an Aristippus, an Antisthenes, a Sakya Mouni, a Mani. Nay, more, Christian men, and eminent saints, with the example of Christ before them, and His Gospels in their hand, could degenerate into some of these conceptions. There is nothing more remarkable than the way in which the teaching of Christ towers not only over the aberrations of Paganism, but even over the sins, negligences, and ignorances of Christian sects and Christian saints [1]. The sensuality of the Hedonists might be matched by the fanaticism of the Antinomians. The absurdity of Plotinus, who blushed that he had a body, may be paralleled by the extravagance of Vianney, who spoke of his body as a corpse [2]. The self-renunciation of the Buddhists may be matched by the fanatic literalism of Origen. Hedonism, Materialism, Asceticism, Mysticism, —what a dominance of error, over what a space of ages do those words imply! and, amid them all, how calm,

---

[1] "The greatest honour is due to Christianity for continually proving its pure and noble origin by coming forth again, *after the great aberrations into which human perversity has led it*, more speedily than was expected, with its primitive special charm as a mission...for the relief of human necessity." Göthe (Stirm, *Apol. d. Christenthums*, p. 193).

[2] "I have sinned against my brother the ass" (*i.e.*, against my body), said St Francis of Assisi. "J'ai un bon *cadavre*, je suis dur," was the reply of Vianney, the remarkable curé d'Ars, when his servant remonstrated with him for eating grass (*Vie*, par l'Abbé Mounin). "Whoever would reside here must bring *his soul only*," wrote De Rancé, the restorer of La Trappe.

how true, how noble, how simple are the few holy and natural principles which Christ revealed! The body is not to be degraded by vile affections, but to be won and possessed in sanctification and honour [1]; not to be crushed by violent asceticism,[2] but to be controlled by quiet discipline; not to be desecrated as a prison, but to be honoured as a shrine. Yes, truly, Christ is also "the Saviour of the body [3]." Consider how His

[1] 1 Thess. iv. 4, εἰδέναι ἕκαστον ὑμῶν τὸ ἑαυτοῦ σκεῦος κτᾶσθαι ἐν ἁγιασμῷ καὶ τιμῇ.

[2] The monks were often wiser in their precepts than in their practice. "If thou art really a servant of Christ," said Benedict to a brother who had chained himself to a rock, "restrain thyself not by a chain of iron, but by the chain of Christ." The reader will be reminded of the reply of the Jesuit father to a weak brother, "*Mangez un bœuf, et soyez Chrétien.*" More than one beautiful tale of saints and hermits shows that they recognized the same truths (see, in Kingsley's *Hermits*, the stories of St Anthony and St Macarius, pp. 97, 147). It is even recognized theoretically in Buddhist Theology. In Captain Rogers's translation of the parables in Buddhaghosha's *Commentary on the Dhammapada*, occurs this passage. "*Not nakedness, not platted hair, not dirt, not fasting or lying on the earth, not rubbing with dust, not sitting motionless, can purify a mortal who has not overcome desires.*" Yet Asceticism had its proper function once. Heine (no prejudiced witness), says, "It was necessary as a healthy reaction against the awful materialism... which threatened to destroy all spiritual nobleness... We recognize the wholesomeness of ascetic discipline when we read Petronius or Apuleius, works which may be regarded as the *pièces justificatives* of Christianity" (quoted by Dr Ward, Manning's *Essays*, I. p. 114). Comte held a similar view, *Phil. Pos.* v. p. 436, *Catech. of Pos. Religion* (tr. Congreve), p. 55. Dr Bridges, *Unity of Comte's Life and Doctrine*, p. 6. Döllinger, *First Age of the Church* (E. Tr.), pp. 344—346. Lecky's *Hist. of European Morals*, I. 117, II. 108, and *passim*. See Col. ii. 21—23.

[3] Eph. v. 23.

revelation of the sacredness of life has put an end to
the dangerous sophisms of the ancient world on the
subject of suicide[1]. Consider how His revelation of
its dignity has inspired the spirit of tenderness and
care. When travelling in the disguise of a beggar, the
scholar Muretus had fallen sick in the hands of strange
physicians; they said, jestingly to one another, "*Fiat
experimentum in corpore vili;*" "*Vilemne animam appellas,*"
he indignantly exclaimed to his astonished auditors:
"*Vilemne animam appellas pro quâ Christus non dedig-
natus est mori?*" "For whom Christ died!"—what mortal
intellect shall measure the full persuasiveness of that
appeal; an appeal for tenderness from others, an appeal
of intense moral force to our own selves! In how different a light does it place those sins against the body
which are the most potent enemies of the dignity of
man! How does our Blessed Lord's innate Divinity
shine forth transcendently in His dealing with sins like
these! The words of human teachers have been too
often like the Pharos-lights which deceived and wrecked
the vessels they were meant to save; but what infinite
delicacy and yet what heart-searching directness, what
uncompromising purity: yet what infinite forbearance is
there in the words of Christ; how sternly inexorable
His requirements, how tenderly infinite His love! The
same lips which said, "*Blessed are the pure in heart,*"

---

[1] See Döllinger, *Gentile and Jew*, I. 357, II. 283, who collects
many passages, to which many more might easily be added. Comte
recognizes the happy and essential service of Christianity in branding
successfully this most anti-social crime. *Phil. Pos.* v. p. 348.

said also, "*Her sins which are many are forgiven her;*" the same which uttered, "*If thy right eye offend thee, pluck it out,*" said also, "*Neither do I condemn thee; go and sin no more*[1]." Yes, He who was purer than the heavens was the most gentle too; and He taught the two doctrines which are more efficacious than all others to cleanse the heart—the Resurrection of the Body, the Indwelling of God's Spirit in the Soul. If, in comparison with the ancient world, or with heathen lands, the society of Christendom be pure; if it be in Christian lands alone that tens of thousands live lives which are healthy and happy and noble because they are uncontaminated by deadly sin, is it not because Christianity, and Christianity alone, can say, Sin not, because the body is for the Lord and the Lord for the body; sin not, because you breathe the air of the Eternal, and live under your Father's eye; sin not, because ye are Temples of the Holy Ghost Who dwelleth in you; sin not, because, as with His mortal body Christ arose, so shall he also rise; and in those bodies whatsoever things ye have done, those same things and not others shall ye receive[2]? Truly, in the words of our great Puritan poet: " He that holds himself in due esteem both for the dignity of God's image upon him, and for the price of his redemption

---

[1] Matt. v. 8; Luke vii. 47; Matt. v. 29; John viii. 11.

[2] 1 Cor. vi. 13; 2 Cor. v. 10; 1 Cor. iii. 16, 17, vi. 19, &c. See Tert. *De Pudicitia*, passim. " Non corpus Christi, non membra Christi, non templum Dei vocabatur, cum veniam mœchiæ consequebatur," 6 ad fin.

which he thinks is visibly marked upon his forehead, accounts himself both a fit person to do the noblest and godliest deeds, and much better worth than to deject and defile, with such a debasement and pollution as sin is, himself so highly ransomed and ennobled to a new friendship and filial relation with God[1]."

2. Of the Intellect and of the Soul I will speak but briefly. Scripture, my brethren, does not contain any regular Psychology, nor were the Gospels intended in any sense to be a formal moral system. We must bear this in mind when we hear the common disparagement that, in the inculcation of this or that virtue, the teaching of Christ was incomplete[2]. It is often, for instance, argued that Christianity gives no special encouragement to the culture of the Intellect[3]. When, as in my text, the Scriptures sum up under

---

[1] Milton, *Reas. of Church Government*.

[2] Prof. F. W. Newman has published a recent pamphlet entitled *Defective Morality of the New Testament*. After carefully reading it, I would say, without meaning any disrespect to the sincere and learned author, that the answer seems to me so simple as to be safely left to every *unbiased* Christian reader of ordinary intelligence. Such remarks as those of Strauss, *New Life of Jesus*, I. 438, so far as they have any truth in them at all, are simply refuted by the consideration that Christianity is not, and was never meant to be, a formal system.

[3] This is a very old accusation against Christianity. Celsus charged Christians with saying κακὸν ἡ ἐν τῷ κόσμῳ σοφία ἀγαθόν δὲ ἡ μωρία. Orig. *c. Cels.* I. p. 8, and VI. p. 282 (ed. 1604), and in several other passages. See Cave, *Prim. Christianity*, I. 3, and *Pref.* Here and there, the language of the *Imitatio Christi* lies open to this charge, *e.g.* I. 2. See a remarkable passage in Dr Newman's *Loss and Gain*, pp. 177, 178.

Body, Soul, and Spirit, the totality of our being, no prominence is given to the mental faculties. Undoubtedly and wisely—nor do I hesitate to say it before a great University, where learning is so justly dear,—Scripture reverses the judgment of the world in making mental culture wholly incommensurate in importance with spiritual growth. The language of St Augustine, "Unhappy the man who knows all those things but is ignorant of these;" the question of the *Imitatio*, "*Scientia sine timore Dei, quid importat*[1]?" the judgment that to have tended on the leper is a higher title to canonization than to have written the *Summa Theologiæ* itself[2], are eminently Christian. To exalt genius would

---

[1] Infelix homo qui sciat ista omnia, te autem nescit; beatus autem qui te scit, etiamsi ista nesciat. Qui vero et te et illa novit, non propter illa beatior, sed propter te solum beatus est." ..Aug. *Conf.* v. 4. "Melior est humilis rusticus qui Deo servit quam superbus philosophus qui se neglecto, cursum cœli considerat." *Imit. Christi*, 1. 82. See Renan, *Étude d'Hist. Rel.* p. 344. Every one will be reminded of Cowper's comparison between Voltaire and the cottager :

"Oh happy peasant ! oh unhappy bard !
His the mere tinsel, hers the sure reward," &c.

"Dieu ne nous demande pas d'être des gens d'esprit, de grandes intelligences, mais il nous demande d'être des hommes de cœur, de grands cœurs." Dupanloup, *Hist. de N. S. Jésus Christ*, p. 6. Among modern philosophers, Kant is conspicuous for his recognition of this truth ; and he used to say that he placed the happiness of future life far more in the intercourse with honest souls—were they even as ignorant as his servant Lampe—than with great minds. All that I have here said finds the strongest and most remarkable confirmation in the views of Comte. See *Phil. Pos.*; Miss Martineau, II. p. 257, 288 ; *Catech. of Pos. Rel.* p. 9 (tr. Congreve).

[2] Sir J. Stephen, *Eccl. Biogr.* I. p. 102.

have been superfluous, because the world was too prone already to that idolatry. On that altar enough of incense had been already heaped. Since the abounding knowledge of the world had, in itself, but served to inflate with insolent self-sufficiency and to dry up with sensual pride [1]; since, without erudition, the heart may be of saintly purity, and without intellectual culture may attain to immortal bliss; to stimulate the intellect was needless, to magnify it would have been pernicious. Not over the portals of Christianity as over the doors of the Academy was ascribed, Μηδεὶς ἀγεωμέτρητος εἰσίτω. Wisdom, not knowledge; goodness, not genius; moral deliverance, not material discovery; the regeneration of the multitude, not the exalting of the few—these were the aims of Christian teaching. The knowledge of mankind needed to be sanctified; it needed to be baptised; it needed to be transfigured from a haughty Philosophy to a humble wisdom, from impotent self-assertion to fruitful life [2]. And, in doing this, Chris-

---

[1] "I am free to confess, my daughter," says Comte, "that hitherto the Positive spirit has been tainted with *the two moral evils which peculiarly wait on knowledge*. It puffs up and it dries the heart, by giving free scope to pride and by turning it from love." *Catech. of Pos. Rel.* p. 72.

[2] There is *a sense* in which the maxim, *Philosophia ancilla Theologiæ*, is profoundly true. In the Vision of Boethius (*De Const. Phil. ad in.*) a noble lady with glowing eyes visits him. On the lower skirt of her garment was the letter Π, on the upper part of it Θ. "There seemed letters between them which rose like the steps of a ladder from one to the other. But the garment had been torn apparently by violence, and some fragments of it carried away." Maurice, *Moral and Metaph. Phil.* II. 17.

tianity by no means degrades the intellect, but subordinates, controls, and so inspires. There have, indeed, been eminent Christians who have spoken of all knowledge with an irritating and an ignorant contempt; but from them and their erring judgments we turn to Christ's own Gospel, which is alone "always true, always sure, always unique, and always consistent with itself." And there we recognize in intellect a talent to be used, in wisdom a blessing to be sought. There echoes the high and loving message, "Son, go work to-day in my vineyard;" there the gentle reproach, "Why stand ye here all the day idle [1]." You therefore, my brethren, who are wise enough to be diligent students, you who are noble enough to feel the charm of high thinking and plain living—and I know that I am speaking to many such—work on with high purpose and fearless faith. Be sure that the "*intellectum valde ama*" of St Augustine expresses the true spirit of your faith. Listen not, my brethren, either to those siren voices which would betray you to the death of self-indulgence, or to the silly sophisms which would stifle your best faculties in the leaden sheet of ignorance. God's vineyard, wherein we are labourers, needs all our toil. God's treasury, wherein we must cast our gifts, needs every mite as well as every talent we possess. We read in an old chronicler a legend of how the Virgin Mother rose clasping a white dove out of a martyr student's tomb, and he ends with the words, "Scholars too are martyrs if they live in purity, and labour

---
[1] Matt. xx. 3, 6, xxi. 28.

with courage[1]." The knowledge which gratifies curiosity, the knowledge which flatters vanity, the knowledge which pushes for precedence, the knowledge which is degraded into a stepping-stone for ambition,—*these* are unblessed of God[2]; but His own spirit will aid the knowledge which is the sister of humility, the handmaid of religion, the counsellor of virtue, the champion of truth. Christianity wrought for the thankless Intellect this high service: she saved it from being paralysed by selfishness, or intoxicated by conceit; she saved it by putting it lower than moral excellence, by depriving it of political supremacy, by opening before it the magnificent arena of social service, by inspiring it with the magnificent enthusiasm of universal love. "You must not only listen but read, you must not only read but think; knowledge," it has been said, "without common sense is folly, without method it is waste, without kindness it is fanaticism, without religion it is death[3];" ay, but—and every page of the New Testament con-

[1] Quoted by Lecky, *Hist. of Eur. Morals*, II. p. 218.
[2] Sunt...qui scire volunt eo tantum fine ut sciant—et turpis curiositas est; et sunt qui scire volunt ut sciantur ipsi, et turpis vanitas est; et sunt item qui scire volunt ut scientiam suam vendant, verbi causâ, pro pecuniâ, pro honoribus, et turpis quæstus est. Sed sunt quoque qui scire volunt ut ædificent, et charitas est, et item qui scire volunt ut ædificentur, et prudentia est." S. Bernard, *Serm.* XXXVI. *super Cant.* p. 604.
[3] From a speech by the late Bp. of Manchester (Dr J. Prince Lee), at the opening of the Bury Athenæum. Cf. S. Bernard, "Ut legeret intelligendi fecit cupiditas; ut intelligeret oratio impetravit; ut impetraret vitæ sanctitas promeruit. Sic cupiat, sic oret, sic vivat qui se proficere velit."

firms the lesson—with common sense it is wisdom; with method it is power; with charity it is beneficence; with religion it is virtue, and life, and peace.

3. But in one last word, let me add that there is something far beyond the well-being of the body, far beyond the cultivation of the mind, it is the salvation of the soul. Here was the greatest part of that finished work. "*He restoreth our souls;* He leadeth us in the paths of righteousness for His Name's sake [1]." And to show that this is all in all, how often have the despised been among His holiest servants, the weakest among His chosen saints; how often have we seen His hand strew dust and ashes over the unhallowed genius and guilty glory of mankind. The world of heathendom, after centuries of philosophy, was emphatically "a world without souls." Now our Blessed Saviour stooped to no idle and degrading discussion whether man had a soul or not; nor did He attempt any futile analysis of what the soul may be. He did not tell us with Empedocles that it was the blood about the heart, or with Aristotle that it was an Entelechy, or with Parmenides that it was the nature of limbs [2]. No; but, simply appealing to the intuitive

[1] Ps. xxiii. 3.

[2] Or (it may be added), with modern materialists, that it is a secretion of phosphorus or the grey substance of the brain. "Die Seele...ist ein Produkt der Entwickelung des Hirns." Vogt, *Physiolog. Briefe.* "Der Gedanke ist eine Bewegung des Stoffes...ohne Phosphor kein Gedanke—auch das Bewusstsein ist nichts als eine Eigenschaft des Stoffes." Moleschott, *Der Kreislauf des Lebens.* See similar passages in Christlieb, *Moderne Zweifel,* p. 160.

sense of men, He told them of the soul's immortality[1] of its accountability, of its divine origin, of its complete redemption, of its Heavenly Father, of its Eternal Life. He uttered to them those solemn words which have rolled to us across the centuries with ever-increasing significance, "*What shall it profit a man, if he shall gain the whole world, and lose his own soul*[2]?" And that word failed not, because it rested not only on a doctrine which men could believe, but on the Life of One whom all could love[3]. It was ardour for *His* service which kindled the glorious devotion of those saints who shine like a river of stars athwart the Church's firmament. *They* are the true glory of Chris-

---

[1] This doctrine of the Immortality of the Soul is claimed also by natural religion. But among the philosophers it was but a wavering hope, a dim imagination, a splendid guess; at best but the uncertain esoteric fancy of a chosen few, not the intense and energetic faith of an entire society. This has been proved too often to need further proof. It will be sufficient here to refer to Archbishop's Whately's Essay *On the Revelation of a Future State* ("On Some Peculiarities of the Christian Religion," Ess. I.). And as ancient philosophers did not discover it, so modern philosophers have given it up. La Mettraie thought that the only chance for the human race lay in materialistic atheism. Cabanis defined the brain as "un estomac qui digère et sécrète des idées." "Mon corps souffre beaucoup," wrote Voltaire to d'Argental (1773); "mon âme, s'il y en a une, ce qui est fort douteuse, vous est tendrement attachée."

[2] Mark viii. 36.

[3] The "categorical imperative" (Duty, Conscience, *Thou must*), as Schiller points out, will fail to command even the obedience of slaves; but thousands will be won by filial obedience and self-renunciation, by "*Be ye holy as I am holy;*" "*Learn of me, for I am meek and lowly of heart.*"

tendom,—*lucentes et ardentes*—the Cherubim of knowledge, and the Seraphim of love. One celebrated collection alone contains the lives of 25,000 of these heroes of unselfishness [1] ; and how high and grand, how full of poetry and nobleness they are! And if, as many tell us,—and as seems, alas, too true,—if, in our refinement and perplexities,—if in our luxury and mammon worship,—if in our despair and faithlessness—the race of these hero souls be past, yet at least the race of the humbler children in God's great family abides. They, thank God, may be counted in their myriads still, and henceforth as heretofore shall the world for which Christ died abound with these beautiful and holy souls. And as the moon can shine only by reflection of the sun, so do these, as they borrow their life and light from the Sun of Righteousness, become the clearest evidence, the predestined issue, the living illustration of their Saviour's work. And while these remain it shall always be believed. Yea, Lord, the enemy may reproach, and the foolish people blaspheme Thy Name, but that Name shall be exalted for ever above every name, for—

" The glorious company of the Apostles praise Thee.
" The goodly fellowship of the Prophets praise Thee.

---

[1] The Bollandist collection. Renan, *Ét. d'Hist. Rel.* 306. 313. Compare the men whom Christianity has canonised with those who won the apotheosis of heathendom, and we shall have some plummet to sound the moral abyss which yawns between the two religions.

"The noble army of Martyrs praise Thee.

"The holy Church throughout all the world doth acknowledge Thee.

"Thou art the King of Glory, O Christ: Thou art the Everlasting Son of the Father."

V.

CHRISTIANITY AND THE RACE.

"Nous tenons à tout, parceque nous venons de Dieu qui est en tout ; rien ne nous est étranger, parceque Dieu n'est étranger nulle part."

LACORDAIRE.

1 COR. III. 22, 23.

"*All are yours; and ye are Christ's; and Christ is God's.*"

THUS far, my brethren, we have watched the material and moral victories of Christianity, and have endeavoured to interpret the powerful and noble witness borne by the full voice of History to Christ the Son of God. But a religion must be judged by its total influences, no less than by its external successes or the virtues of its individual believers; and therefore it still remains to show—in a manner however imperfect and fragmentary—that Christianity has rendered clearer and brighter the whole atmosphere of life; that it has been to Christian nations a blessing no less inestimable than it has been to Christian men.

And this is all the more necessary, because, but for an overruling Providence, the absorbing intensity of religious convictions not only *might*, but undoubtedly *would* have restrained, or even nullified the political and social influence of our faith. We can indeed hardly wonder that, under the strong dominion of personal religion, the minds of many have been unable to think

of anything beyond,—have failed to realise the existence
of any entity except their souls and God. Mere isolated
fragments of religious truth have covered their limited
vision, even as the entire horizon may be concealed by
the smallest object held close to the pupil of the eye.
We are told of an illiterate hermit named Pambos, that,
coming to be taught a Psalm, he learnt the single verse,
"I said, I will take heed to my ways that I offend
not with my tongue ;" and when asked six months, and
again many years afterwards, why he did not come to
learn another, he replied that he had never been able
truly to master this[1]. It has been the same with other
truths; nor is it strange that when men contemplated
exclusively the awe-inspiring thoughts of Immortality and
the Judgment to come, they could have been ready to
take refuge from themselves in fiery deserts or seaside
caves, and to abandon every object and every interest
except the salvation of their individual souls[2]. Espe-

[1] Socrates, *H. E.* IV. 23, quoted by Lecky, *Hist. of Europ. Morals*, II. p. 123.

[2] "The Church," says Dr. Newman, "regards this world and all that is in it as a mere shade, as dust and ashes, compared with the value of one single soul. She holds...that it were far better for sun and moon to drop from heaven, for the earth to fail, and for all the many millions who are on it to die of starvation in extremest agony, as far as temporal affliction goes, than that one soul, I will not say, should be lost, but should commit one single venial sin." *Anglican Difficulties*, p. 48. It is a useless exercise of the imagination to put such impossible hypotheses ; and, at any rate, to reckon the heinousness of sin by this kind of calculus is wholly unscriptural. It is like the exaggerated language of Jerome—that it was better that Rome should be devastated with sword and flame by the barbarians then that one Christian should lose her virginity.

cially was this the case, when, to the solemnity of such
beliefs, was added the remorse and anguish of a guilty
conscience.

> "A spotless child sleeps on the flowery moss .
> 'Tis well for him—but when a guilty man,
> Envying such slumber, may desire to put
> His guilt away—can he return to rest
> At once by lying there? our sires knew well
> The fitting way for such;—dark cells; dim lamps,
> A stony floor one may writhe on like a worm,
> No mossy pillow blue with violets[1]."

The gloomy heresies of Gnostic and Manichee, the unnatural and maddening penances of hermit and Stylite,
the entire impulse to asceticism and monastic Christianity, had their origin in this absorbing aim at personal deliverance. And to this day large sections of the Christian
Church, in the words of their formulæ—though to a less
extent, thank God, in the lives of their children—dwell
too prominently and persistently on the doctrine that
man's one object in this world is to save his soul[1]. Take
even the *Imitatio Christi;* who has not benefited by the

[1] Browning, *Paracelsus*.
[2] "Why did God make you? To know Him, love Him, and serve Him in this world and be happy with Him in the next." *Rom. Cath. Catech.* "Homo creatus est ut laudet Deum, eique serviat, et per hæc salvet animam suam." St Ignat. *Exercises.* (Manning, *Essays*, 2nd Series, p. 29.) This is, of course, true; but it is a pity that the definition of service to God is not made definitely to include the service to man. The passage in Dr. Newman's *Apologia*, in which he says that the effect of "early" teaching on his mind had been to deepen mistrust of material phenomena, and "to make him rest in the thought of two, and two only, supreme and unanimously self-evident beings—myself and God," has become famous. Dr Westcott has shown how scepticism at once

light and heat, the glowing beauty and intense devotion of that unrivalled Epos of the Soul's love? And yet, as has forcibly been pointed out, never was there a more glaring misnomer than the title of the book. It was Christ's glorious originality that He went about doing good; it was His New Commandment, " Ye must love one another :" yet both His continual practice, and His strongest precept, are, in this book, all but totally ignored[1]. Yes, the *Imitatio Christi* is a book, which in its pictures of personal holiness, of absolute self-denial, of passionate devotion, no other religion but Christianity could have produced; and yet had Christianity been no more than this, it would indeed have been amenable to the charge, now falsely brought against it, that its views are anti-industrial, its tendency antisocial, its motives egotistic[2]. It might, here and there, have inspired some pure and devoted solitary, but it could never have reformed society, or civilized the world. It would have perished in some lonely laura of desert cœnobites, or some dead sect upon the Dead Sea shore.

But Christianity is more and greater than the *Imi-*

seizes the abandoned ground of Society and Science. *Aspects of Positivism in Rel. to Christianity;* Contemp. Rev. VIII. p. 371.

[1] This fact is admirably developed in Milman, *Lat. Christianity*, VI. p. 484. His language, however, requires some slight modification.

[2] This charge "infructuosi in negotiis dicimur," is constantly refuted in the Fathers. Orig. *c. Cels.* VIII. 73; Tert. *Apol.* 42; Lactant. *Div. Inst.* V. 22; Arnobius, *Adv. Nat.* II. *ad f.* "The Roman rulers," says Comte, "felt no hesitation in rejecting, as the enemy of the human race, a provisional religion which considered perfection as consisting in an *entire concentration upon heavenly objects.*" *Cat. of Pos. Rel.*

tatio, and the Apostles set before mankind a grander object than even personal salvation. " Perish my name," cried Danton, "but let France be free." Men have admired the splendid self-sacrifice of the utterance, who forgot to admire the Source whence that spirit came. Moses was never greater, never more worthy to be an heroic lawgiver, than when from that giant heart of his burst forth the cry, " If thou wilt forgive their sin— and if not, blot me, I pray thee, out of the book that thou hast written." St Paul was never nobler, never more like his Lord, than when, in language which ever since has been the stumbling-block of all feeble Christians, he exclaimed that he wished himself accursed from God for his brethren, his kinsmen according to the flesh. The love which Christ taught, was a love not inspired by individual prudence, but destined for social use. Reversing the narrow intolerance of an ambitious theology, he valued charity far above orthodoxy[1], and placed a tender nature far higher than a correct belief. And hence the motto, 'No man for himself, every man for all[2],' expresses the very ideal of a Christian society; it will abound in purity, charity, devotion, conquest of self, activity for others; its true members will be " not slothful in business, fervent in spirit, serving the Lord." And this is why Christianity achieved not only an individual deliverance but a social restitution; this is

---

[1] " Leave there thy gift before the altar, and go thy way; *first* be reconciled to thy brother, and then come and offer thy gift." Matt. v. 24.

[2] Herder.

why it became the Palingenesia of a dead and miserable world. For Antiquity had never honoured man as man, but only as he was adorned by the accidents of wealth or beauty, intellect or rank. That intensified definition of the tyrant's creed, the

"Humanum paucis vivit genus"

of Lucan, expressed their steady conviction; humanity in their eyes had no higher destiny than to be the footstool for a few. But Christ came to love, as none had ever loved, those whom none had ever loved as yet. He was the protector of children, the healer of the sick, the friend of the sinful, the teacher of the ignorant, the seeker of the wandering, the Saviour of the lost. Seen in the light of the Incarnation and the Resurrection, all life, even the humblest, was transfigured as by a glory from heaven. Man as man, and apart from every adventitious or ennobling circumstance, became a holy and a royal thing[1]. Paganism degraded woman; Christ found among women, even the fallen and the sinful, His chosen ministers. Paganism had neglected children universally, had degraded them in myriads, had murdered them wholesale; Christ made them the types of loving humility, and "flung the desecrator of their innocence, with a millstone round his neck, into the sea[2]." Paganism had oppressed the people with shameful bondage

---

[1] "Tu, Homo, tantum nomen si te scias." Aug.
[2] Infanticide and similar crimes are still rife throughout the East. Modern philosophers, from Voltaire down to the Comtists, are fond of pointing China to us as an example of what civilisation without Christianity can do. The Comte de Beauvoir (*Voy. autour*

and sneered at them with insolent contempt: Christ sprang from the midst of them, and made the meanest of them who believed in Him children of God and inheritors of heaven. Paganism, criminal itself, was yet to the criminal most pitilessly cruel: Christ was to sinners a Saviour and a friend[1]. The two beneficent spirits of Love and Liberty at once sprang into life from His teaching—two spirits which became the guardian angels of suffering humanity, and sheltered it more and more beneath their healing wings.

1. The Pagan world laboured under a triple curse—the curse of corruption, the curse of cruelty, the curse of slavery. At its corruption we have glanced already. But lust, as usual, was hard by hate, and the spirit of *cruelty* also had pervaded every region of its life:

---

du Monde), in one evening walk out of Canton, found *seven* abandoned babies, some purposely wounded, all blue and dying of cold. The Sisters of Charity go out with a great basket to save all they can; in one *year* they picked up 4000, most of them too far gone to be revived!

[1] "Ces faiblesses sont la force de l'Eglise, qui a fait alliance avec elles, et les a prises sous sa protection en se mettant sous la leur. Cette alliance a changé la face de la société." Lacordaire, *Conférences*, 1846, p. 356. "Tous les systèmes les plus vastes, les plus progressifs que la sagesse humaine a mis au jour, et qu'elle a voulu substituer à la religion, *n'ont jamais pu intéresser que les savants, ou les ambitieux, ou tout au plus les heureux du monde*. Mais la grande majorité du genre humain ne sera jamais dans ces catégories. *La grande majorité des hommes est souffrante*, souffrante des douleurs morales autant que de maux physiques...or lequel de ces systèmes a jamais consolé un cœur affligé, peuplé un cœur désert? lequel de ces docteurs a jamais enseigné à essuyer une larme?" Montalembert, *Ste Eliz. d' Hongroie*, 1. p. 155.

but, from the hour when through the starlight rang the
first angelic carol which told that Christ was born,
from that hour began the death-knell to every Satanic
tyranny and every tolerated crime. It was the glory
of Athens that she alone had reared a solitary altar
to Pity; but Christ raised an altar to Pity in every
Christian heart. The philosophers had derided as foi-
bles both compassion and almsgiving; but to feed the
hungry, to clothe the naked, to teach the ignorant, to
bring light into the prison, to strike the fetters off the
slave—these had been among the simplest and earliest
lessons of the Christian's faith. That chord of pathos
which the Gospel had struck vibrated into a noble
music. "For the first time," says the historian of Rationalism, "the aureole of sanctity encircled the brow of
sorrow, and invested it with a mysterious charm [1]." The
hardness which had enabled even women to gloat over
the agonies of the dying gladiator or the tortures of the
slave, became now a sign of exceptional degradation:
and when the obscure monk, Telemachus, had faced
the furious populace, and bought by his death the
abolition of those cruel sports [2], the amphitheatres—
whose circle had been reddened so often with the
blood of martyrs—were suffered to crumble into un-
interrupted decay. But, side by side with the damning

[1] Lecky, *Hist. of Eur. Rational.* II. p. 266.

[2] Jan. 1, A.D. 404, at the celebration of the 6th consulship of
Honorius. Theodoret. *H. E.* v. 26; Gibbon, III. 70, 71 (ed.
Milman). The fathers and Christian writers had vainly uttered
against these games their strongest denunciations. Lact. *Div Instt.*
VI. 20; Prudent. *c. Symm.* II. 1121.

witness of their huge ruins, there arose ornaments more splendid than if there had been a Coliseum in every valley and a Parthenon on every hill—the Retreats and Asylums, the Hospitals and Orphanages, of which heathen selfishness had never dreamed. Who can sum up the amount of misery which these institutions have alleviated or removed? He who has sat, on some quiet evening, among the shattered seats at the summit of the Coliseum, and heard, stealing upwards through the calm air, the hymns of the Fratres Misericordiæ, as they perform in that enormous area the touching service of the *Via Crucis,*—he who, on that sod which once reeked with the blood of 10,000 gladiators[1], has seen the Roman Princesses kneeling humbly side by side with the peasant woman on the green grass before the painted records of their Saviour's agony,—can best realise, by one startling contrast, the gulf which yawns between the brutalities of a sanguinary Paganism and the tender mercy of the religion of our Lord.

2. Hardly less memorable was the service which Christianity achieved by wiping out the curse of *slavery*.

[1] The number said to have been displayed by Trajan on 123 holidays. See Lecky, *Hist. of Eur. Morals*, I. pp. 37, 104, 287, &c. It is needless to quote any further testimonies on a subject so well known, but it is worth while to quote the oath of gladiators —sublime in its atrocity—preserved in Petronius: "In verba Eumolpi sacramentum juravimus, *uri, vinciri, verberari, ferroque, necari,* et quicquid aliud Eumolpus jussisset, tanquam legitimi gladiatores, domino corpora animasque religiosissime addicimus." Cf. Sen. Ep. 7, " mera homicidia sunt." The letter contains a terrible picture. See Chastel, *Sur l'Influence de la Charité durant les premiers Siècles*—(crowned by the French Academy in 1852).

Philosophers with pernicious ingenuity had not only tolerated slavery as inevitable, but had defended it as right. Plato had not condemned, Aristotle had supported, Cicero had excused it; centuries afterwards Libanius argued in its favour, and Julian—however compassionate—had not taken one step to put it down. And yet nothing can be more certain than that slavery has been the disgrace and ruin of every nation that practised it, crushing the enslaved masses, weakening the tyrannous minority[1], corrupting both. Stigmatising labour, it fostered a dissolute sloth; destroying the middle classes, it avenged itself by rendering most liable to unpitied slavery the nations that have most multiplied their slaves. Hence, as the Roman historian said of Greece, and as the Gothic historian might no less truthfully have said of Rome, *Introisse victoria fuit.* Now Christianity did not at once abolish slavery[2]—

[1] Among the 1,200,000 inhabitants of Rome in Cicero's time, there *were scarcely* 2000 *proprietors.* " *Vix esse duo millia hominum qui rem habent.*" Cic. *de Off.* II. 21. It is reckoned that in the entire empire there must have been 60,000,000 slaves. Le Maistre, *Du Pape,* I. p. 283. There is scarcely one Roman writer who does not furnish some fatal evidence as to the treatment and estimation of slaves from Plautus down to Ammianus Marcellinus, XIV. 6. It is summed up in the one sentence of Seneca, "In servos *superbissimi, crudelissimi, contumeliosissimi sumus.*" *Ep.* 47. See too Cic. *de Rep.* 14, 23; Juv. *Sat.* III. 14, and the curious debate in Tac. *Ann.* XIV. 43. See too Waller, *Hist. de l'Esclavage dans l'Antiquité.*

[2] This was an old reproach against Christianity, and was answered by Chrysost. *ad* I *Cor.* Hom. XIX. "Through the vista of history we see slavery and its pagan theory of two races fall before the holy word of Jesus—All men are the children of God."

which would have been revolutionary and impossible—
but, by sapping its very foundations, rendered certain
its final abolition. For the Church, interpreting the
deeds and words of her Divine Founder, declared, with
a voice of unmistakable majesty, that the φύσει δοῦλοι
were fictions of man's tyrannous and selfish pride [1],
and that each man is just as great as he is in God's
sight, and never greater [2]. It is true that self-interest
has attempted to wrest the New Testament in its own
favour, but so futile has been the effort that the most
prejudiced historians do not deny that to Christianity
mainly the abolition of slavery was due. It preached
emancipation as a duty, and rewarded it as a privilege;
it elevated the slave into a serf, ennobled by the sense
of mutual obligations between his seigneur and himself,
and then, flinging over him a shield of adamant, it told
the proudest baron who dared to do him wrong that
he did so at the peril of his soul [3]. And thus it removed from labour, both manual and agricultural, the
unworthy brand of shame. Greeks and Romans spoke

Mazzini, *Works*, VI. 99; Lecky, *Hist. of Rational.* II. 258; Troplong, *De l'Influence du Christ. sur le Droit Civil*, p. 10; Ozanam, *Hist. of Fifth Cent.* I. 147 (E. tr.); M. H. Reynald, *Rech. sur ce qui manquait à la Liberté dans les Rép. anc.* p. 177; Bunsen, *Gott in der Gesch.* V. 3.

[1] φύσει μὲν οὖν διώρισται τὸ θῆλυ καὶ τὸ δοῦλον. Arist. comp. Politics, I. 2, with Col. iii. 11. πολέμιοι φύσει. Plat. *Rep.* V. p. 470. See a remarkable passage in Plutarch, *De fort. Alex.*, and Merivale, *Conv. of Rom. Emp.* p. 48. [2] St Francis of Assisi.

[3] "In an age when the weak were prostrate at the feet of the strong, who was there but the Church to plead to the strong for the weak?" Mill, *Dissert.* II. 155.

of artisans and barbarians with contemptuous disgust;
but Christians never forgot that their Lord and Master
had chosen the earthly position of a barbarian and an
artisan [1]. And hence the fathers preached in their
noblest tones the duty and the dignity of honourable
toil. The proudest Bishops were not ashamed to dig;
a Benedict worked six hours a day with hoe and spade;
a Becket helped regularly to reap the fields. The monks
at once practised labour, and ennobled and protected
it [2]. The towns and the middle classes grew up under
their shelter. *Laborare et orare* became the motto of
Christian life. " *Work*," said De Rancé, to his poverty-
stricken and disheartened followers at La Trappe, "work
will subdue all regrets;" and the crock of gold which
in a few moments tinkled under his vigorous spade
did but typify the blessing and the usefulness of toil.
To teach that blessedness has ever been the Church's
duty; nor will that duty cease till she has trained all
her sons to the belief that a life of mere amusement
is dishonourable and disgraceful; that "to consume
much and to produce little, to sit down at the feast of

[1] The constant *taunt* against Christianity as to the humility and obscurity of its origin (δέκα ναύτας καὶ τελώνας τοὺς ἐξωλεστάτους μόνους εἷλε, Orig. *c. Cels.* II. 46 ; μειράκια καὶ οἰκοτρίβων ὄχλον καὶ ἀνοήτων ἀνθρώπων ὅμιλον, *Id.* III. 50) was in reality at once its *glory* and its *evidence*.

[2] "They knew," says Mr Mill, of the Benedictines, "and taught that temporal work may be a spiritual exercise ; and, protected by their sacred character from depredation, they set the first example to Europe of industry conducted on a large scale by free labour." Mill, *Dissertations*, II. 154. See too Lecky, *Hist. of Rational.* II. 261 seqq.

life, and to depart without paying the reckoning [1]," is a sin too deeply-seated to be successfully gilded over by the mere profession of a Christian faith.

If then we look—not at the Christianity of feeble practices and superstitious formulæ—but at Christianity in its freest action and purest essence, we see that it wiped out the worst curses of Heathendom. Nor was this the only way in which, beyond all dispute, it laid the very foundation of that system to which, with its magnificent inheritance of progressive institutions and settled aims, we give the vague name of Modern Civilization[2]. I trust that one rapid final glance will determine our conviction that Intellectually, Socially, Politically it was and is the aim, and by God's especial blessing the successful aim of Christianity, to guide and to glorify the present and the future destinies of man.

I. *Intellectually* her work was less direct and immediate than in the other spheres; and yet how vast it was. To begin with Language itself, how has Chris-

[1] Lord Derby, *Speech at Glasgow.*

[2] "Toutes les diverses branches essentielles de la morale universelle ont reçu du catholicisme (M. Comte means from Christianity, but prefers the other term) des améliorations capitales..." Comte, *Phil. Pos.* v. 435. "Le Christianisme a été sur tous les points le puissant auxiliaire des idées de civilisation et de progrès." Troplong, p. 145. "Wir sind mit unserer ganzen Zeit aus dem Boden des Christenthums niedergestellt und von ihm ausgegangen." Fichte, *Anweisung zum seligen Leben.* See too Schmidt, *Sur la Société civile dans le Monde romain*, 1853. "Among the improvers of the ideal of humanity," even Strauss admits, "Jesus stands at all events in the first class." *New Life of Jesus*, II. 437. "Catholicism *laid the very foundations of modern civilization.*" Lecky, *Hist. of Rat.* II. 32.

tianity enriched, preserved, inspired it. How many languages, like the Gothic, Cornish, Old Prussian, Saxon and Bulgarian, are solely preserved in fragments of scriptural and ecclesiastical documents; how many more, like the German and the English, have been fixed and elevated by versions of the Bible; how many more, of the deepest interest for the student of humanity, have been solely made known to us, in every region of the globe, by missionary research[1]? In Art again, which Greece and Rome had elaborated to such perfection of beauty, but degraded by such immorality of aim[2], how deep and salutary was the influence of our faith. Recall, however slightly, the greatest names of art—in Painting, a Tintoretto and a Raphael; in Architecture, a Brunelleschi and a Giotto; in Sculpture, a Ghiberti and a Michael Angelo; in Music, a Handel and a Mozart :—recall the loveliest creations of artistic genius, the resplendent mosaics of the great Italian basilicas, the Transfiguration, or the Madonna di San Sisto, the great cathedrals of Normandy and of England, the dome of Michael Angelo or the Campanile of Florence, the statues of Moses at Rome, or the Apostles at Copenhagen, the musical notation, and the development of harmony, and the invention

---

[1] "Elle est traduite en plus de cent trente cinq langues, et comme jadis chez les Goths d'Ulphilas, *elle a créé chez plus d'un peuple l'alphabet*, la lecture, et l'écriture." Reville (quoted Luthardt, *Heilswahrheiten*, p. 239).

[2] See Plin. *II. N.* 36. 5; Aug. *Civ. Dei*, II. 7; Clem. *Strom.* V. 5; *Protrept.* II: *Phil. Pos.* V. 465; Ozanam, II. ch. viii.

of the organ to lend new majesty to holy worship, and you will see at once the æsthetic influence of Christian faith. Or again, in Literature, enumerate the very greatest glories of eighteen Christian centuries, and consider whether they be not the certain and the natural outcome of purely Christian influences [1]. The *Civitas Dei*, the *Divina Commedia*, the *Summa Theologiæ*, the *Imitatio Christi*, the *Novum Organum*, the *Plays* of Shakespeare, the *Paradise Lost*, the *Pilgrim's Progress*, the *In Memoriam*—are not these severally matchless in their kind, and are they not works of which any one would have been impossible to Paganism, and to which heaven and earth have alike contributed [2]? Is there one work in all immoral, in all unchristian literature which you would match with these? Will you set the *Confessions* of Rousseau [3] side by side with the *Confessions* of St Augustine, or compare Paine's *Age*

---

[1] It is almost superfluous to allude to the services of the Reformers in favour of schools and classical learning. "That the clergy were the preservers of all letters and all culture, of the writings and even the traditions of literary antiquity, is too evident to have been ever disputed. But for them there would have been a complete break in Western Europe between the ancient and modern world." Mill, *Dissert.* II. 154.

[2] Ozanam (*Civiliz. in VIth Cent.* II. 44) calls the *Divina Commedia* "a poem that rang with the groans of earth and the hymns of heaven"—
"Poema sacro
A cui ha porto man cielo e terra."

[3] Rousseau has uttered many wise and noble sentiments; but his political negativism would have led to a most deplorable and antisocial retrogression; and morally it *did* lead to a brutal preponderance of the passions over the reason. Comte, *Phil. Pos.* v. 772.

of Reason with Hooker's *Ecclesiastical Polity?* Does not the history of all literature prove that not even the brightest wit or the keenest genius—not even the stately eloquence of Bolingbroke, or the universal learning of Diderot, or the glowing imagination of Byron, or the flashing witticisms of Voltaire—can save the writings of men, however gifted, from perishing of inevitable decay, if they sin against the rules of morality, or are aimed against the principles of faith?

II. Yet *Socially* the work of Christianity was more inestimable still. The vast moral revolution which it wrought may be summed up in this sentence,—that it founded the entire relations between man and man not, as heathendom had done, on selfishness, but on the new basis of universal love. The ideal of the Christian family, an ideal lovelier and happier· than any which the world has ever known, is the direct creation of Christianity. '*Familia*,' to the ear of a Roman, meant a multitude of idle, corrupt, and corrupting slaves, kept in subjection by the cross and the *ergastulum*, ready for any treachery, and reeking with every vice. It meant a despot who could kill his slaves when they were aged, and expose his children when they were born; it meant matrons among whom virtue was rare, divorces frequent, remarriage easy, and who, from no stronger motive than that of vanity, would sacrifice the lives of their infants yet unborn; it meant children spectators from their infancy of insolence and cruelty, servility and sin. But the new faith, while it sanctioned the authority of parents, checked their despotism; it made marriage sacred and indissoluble; it encircled the position of womanhood with all that was pure and divine, and tender, in the names of mother and of wife. Well might the Pagan orator exclaim with envy, "What women these Christians have[1]!" A Phœbe and a Priscilla, a Fabiola and a Pulcheria, a Paula and a Eustochia, a Monica and a Perpetua, a Placilla and a Gorgonia were new phenomena to the Pagan world. For families in which, like sheltered flowers, spring up all that is purest and sweetest in human lives; for marriage exalted to an almost sacramental dignity; for all that circle of heavenly blessings which result from a common self-sacrifice; for that beautiful unison of noble manhood, stainless womanhood, joyous infancy, and uncontaminated youth; in one word, for all that there is of divinity and sweetness in the one word *Home;* for this—to an extent which we can hardly realise—we are indebted to Christianity alone[2].

III. Again, *Politically*, how immense and how

---

[1] See Chrys. *ad Vid. Jun.;* Cave, *Prim. Christianity*, II. 5. What Pagan women were may be seen from Juv. *Sat.* IV.; Tac. *Ann.* XV. 32, 37, XII. 53, II. 85. Seneca draws a beautiful picture of his mother Helvia, but he ascribes to her as virtues the absence of many common and atrocious vices. Their best ideal was of the somewhat poor "domi mansit, lanam fecit" type; and it was clear that the Greeks admired an Ismene more than an Antigone. See the Speech of Pericles, Thuc. II. 45.

[2] This entire subject has been admirably treated by Comte, "Ce soin préponderant du catholicisme pour la morale domestique a eu tant d'admirables résultats que leur analyse sommaire ne saurait être indiquée ici." *Phil. Pos.* V. 439.

beneficent was its direct action[1]. i. Consider how great was the problem solved by the fundamental separation, yet co-ordinate action of Church and State. The old Greek Utopias were here realized, not by a Pedantocracy of unpractical philosophers, but by a due subordination of the intellect to social activity, and by rendering the entire commonwealth of empires amenable to a central spiritual power. It was thus that morality, which is ever growing in political force, was first definitely infused into civil governments[2], and its immediate effect was to mollify all anarchical elements, to interpose a truce of God between the oppressor and the oppressed,

---

[1] To Mr Church's remark that "during the first ten centuries Christianity had hardly leavened society at all," I oppose Mr Lecky, *Hist. of Rational.* II. 32, 255, 288, and Comte, *Phil. Pos.* v. 335—341. He says that during ten centuries, from St Paul to Hildebrand, the elaboration of the ecclesiastical system—the *chef d'œuvre* of human wisdom—was aided by all the greatest men of those centuries (the Augustines, Jeromes, Gregories, &c.), and that if sometimes interrupted "par l'ombrageuse médiocrité des rois, fut presque toujours hautement secondée par tous les souverains doués d'un vrai génie politique." v. 388. "The separation of temporal and spiritual," says M. Guizot, "is founded on the idea that material force had no right, no hold over the mind, over civilization, over truth." "Enormous as have been the sins of the Catholic Church," adds Mr Mill, "in the way of intolerance, her assertion of this truth has done more for human freedom than all the fires she enkindled to destroy it." *Dissert.* II. 243.

[2] "Le Christianisme donna son caractère à la jurisprudence, car l'Empire a toujours eu du rapport avec le sacerdoce. *On peut voir le code Theodosien qui n'est qu'une compilation des ordonnances des empereurs chrétiens.*" Montesquieu, *Esprit des Lois*, XIII. 21; Troplong, *Influence du Christianisme sur le Droit Civil*, p. 10; Ozanam, *Hist. of Civil. in Vth Cent.* I. 154 (E. tr.).

and in an age of blood and iron to make the sword fall before the cross. ii. Again, consider the great idea of Unity—the Solidarity of Peoples—the strong bond between the members of a common Christendom. The great fabric of International Law was built upon the conception that all nationalities, however isolated or antagonistic, were fused into the higher unity of a dominant Church, of which even the barbarous tribes of unexplored continents were regarded as the natural subjects. "Sirs, ye are brethren," was the voice of Christendom to warring kings. It was a magnificent faith. Henceforth the contemptuous exclusiveness of Greece, the cunning, cruel, tortuous policy of Rome [1], fell absolutely under the ban. Henceforth there were no "natural enemies;" no treating of conquered barbarians like animals or plants; no selfish sacrifice of the ignorant many to the illuminated few. Priests had begun their sacrifices with the cry " *Procul este profani*," but the true voice of Christianity was " Come unto me." The Philosophers had never dreamed of it, but the real Unity of Mankind, revealed by the Incarnation of the Son of God, had been first proclaimed, amid a thousand perils, by the wandering tent-maker ; and the full Universality of the Gospel had been first revealed to the Galilæan fisherman as he slept at noonday on the tanner's roof. To realize this Unity, to effect this Universality, was the great mission of the Church. She did not discourage Patriotism, but by supplementing it with the

[1] Nowhere more acutely exposed than in Montesquieu, *Grandeur et Décadence*.

conception of our common humanity she rendered it intenser and more sublime [1]. The ancients had had mysteries and secret doctrines, but the whole of Christianity was open to her very meanest son : the heathen had adored local divinities and gods of the profession and the class, but the Saviour whom Christians worshipped was the Saviour of the world.   iii. Once more, consider what the Church did for Education. Her ten thousand monasteries kept alive and transmitted that torch of learning which otherwise would have been extinguished long before. A religious education, incomparably superior to the mere athleticism of the noble's hall, was extended to the meanest serf who wished for it [2]. This fact alone, by proclaiming the dignity of the Individual, elevated the entire hopes and destinies of the race. The humanizing machinery of Schools and Uni-

[1] *Unam omnium rempublicam agnoscimus, mundum.* Tert. *Apol.* 34. Similarly the higher-minded even of the Jews held that the high priest's sacrifices were offered for the whole world. Philo, *De Monarchia*, II. 825.

[2] Christianity has often been accused of discouraging Patriotism ; the charge would be infinitely more true of Philosophy. Hegel, taking the MS. of his first book to the printer on the day of the battle of Jena ; Humboldt calmly working in his study while a revolution was raging in the streets ; Göthe apparently undisturbed by, and indifferent to, the invasion of his country—does any one think their conduct more Christian than that of Fichte in rousing his audience to fight for fatherland ? "The artist Göthe looked on unmoved : his heart knew no responsive throb to the emotion that shook his country." Mazzini, *Works*, VI. 99. Christianity has never been an enemy to national feeling, though she has infused into Christendom "a bond of unity which is *superior* to the divisions of nationhood." Lecky, *Hist. of Rat.* II. 32.

versities, the civilizing propaganda of missionary zeal, were they not due to her? And, more than this, her very existence was a living education: it showed that the successive ages were not sporadic and accidental scenes, but were continuous and coherent acts in the one great drama. In Christendom the yearnings of the past were fulfilled, the direction of the future determined. In dim but magnificent procession, "the giant forms of empires on their way to ruin" had each ceded to *her* their sceptres, bequeathed to *her* their gifts. There was no cleft between Pagan and Christian; no break between Jerusalem and Rome. The Poetry, the Patriotism, the Tolerance of Heathendom, were incorporated with the Holiness, the Universality, the Hopes of the one true faith[1]. Life became one broad rejoicing river, whose tributaries, once severed, were now united; and whose majestic stream, without one break in its continuity, flowed on, under the common sunlight, from its source beneath the Throne of God.

Thus then does History "set to her seal that God is true." And whence, my brethren, in the face of these glorious facts, and a thousand more on which it is impossible to dwell—whence then arises the strange antagonism to Christianity? In reading works hostile to our faith[2], I find that, besides the disbelief in the

---

See Ozanam, I. 68; Comte, v. 350.

[2] It has never been a tradition among Christians to ignore the criticism of objectors. Aug. *Civ. Dei*, *Pref.* "Verumtamen cognosce quid eos contra moveat, atque rescribe ut vel epistolis vel libris, si adjuverit Deus, ad omnia respondere curemus."

Supernatural, and the consequent rejection of the Divinity of Christ—most of their criticisms may be summed up under the three broad calumnies, that Christianity is irreconcilable with Science, opposed to Liberty, and superseded by Civilization. It would be an easy task, my brethren, did time permit, to rend these charges to pieces and fling them to the four winds. All that can now be said is this, that, (1) as regards Science, if, above all things, it requires courage, honesty, enthusiasm, we too exclaim with all the emphasis of impassioned and believing prayer ἐν δὲ φάει καὶ ὀλέσσον. To all true Religion, as to all true Science, the Universe is an open book of revelation, whose divine hieroglyphics are decipherable by toil, and every fresh discovery is but a fresh fact to be recorded and co-ordinated with those which we already know. But Science and Faith must ever be united, they are the two wings whereby alone we can soar to the knowledge of God. And, believe me, if there be a theological, there is also such a thing as a scientific narrowness[1] : there is a noble Science, and there is a Science inflated and ignorant, and, little as their authors knew of the sublimest laws of nature, yet this kind of Science is a thing as much lower than the Pentateuch or the Book of Psalms, as a treatise of Astronomy, however accurate, is a smaller thing than the midnight with all its stars.

[1] "Which denies the power of revelation innate in man, in order to date the discovery of truth from the meagre labours upon a fragment of creation studied by one single faculty of the mind." Mazzini, *Fortn. Rev.* p. 730 (June, 1870).

(2) And who dares to say that our faith is an enemy to Liberty? To that liberty indeed which is but an ill-disguised name for brutal license—to that liberty which holds in her right hand a civic wreath, in her left a human head—to that liberty which has "for her lullaby the carmagnole, and for her toy the guillotine," she *is* an enemy. But not even in the men of Marathon, or of Thermopylæ, did genuine Freedom find firmer or more unflinching friends than in the Church of Christ[1]. Athens had her slaves, Sparta her Helots, Rome her proletariat, Hindostan her Pariahs, but to the Church all men were brothers, and in her language alone the greatest Queen is but "this woman," and the lordliest Emperor "this man;" nor did she ever alter one single syllable of her funeral offices, whether they were read over the open grave of a Pauper or of a Prince. And did Harmodius or Timoleon, did a Scævola or a Brutus ever face despots more bravely than her sons? St John before Herod, St Paul before Nero; Lucifer of Cagliari telling Constantine that he could not respect his diadems, earrings, and bracelets when it was a question of duty towards God; St Ambrose repulsing Theo-

---

[1] In the Middle Ages the Church was "the chief refuge and hope of oppressed humanity." Mill, *Dissert.* II. 293. "The liberties of the Church in that age were the liberties of mankind." Michelet, *Hist. de France*, II. 343. We owe to the Church "the idea of the Unity of the human family, and *of the equality and emancipation of souls.*" Mazzini, *Letter to Œcumen. Council* (*Fortn. Rev.* June, 1870, p. 737). In this letter Mazzini sums up with remarkable eloquence and candour the past services of the Church.

dosius from the cathedral gates of Milan, St Columbanus rebuking King Thierry for his incontinence, St Anselm braving the anger of the violent and haughty Rufus; these scenes, and a hundred like them, are the grandest comment on the true and noble words of Melanchthon, *Tyrannis est inimica Ecclesiæ* [1].

[1] Melanchthon, *De abusibus emendandis*. On the other hand, sceptics have been amongst the most selfish flatterers of tyrants— witness the conduct of Hobbes to Charles II., and Voltaire telling Catherine II. his regret that she has "a name which is also inscribed in the vulgar calendar!" Hard indeed would be the lot of the people if the universal selfishness of disbelief prevailed. Voltaire called them "*un composé d'ours et de singes*," and he even advised Frederic II. to condescend to leave religion to "*la canaille, qui n'est pas digne d'être éclairée, et à laquelle tous les jougs sont propres.*" Far different has been the conduct and the language of that Church to which the people have often been so ungrateful. It was in the Church alone that a serf's son might rise not only to be the equal of barons, but to be the superior of kings; in English history Longchamps, Grostête, Wolsey and others, were all sons of peasants; and in Papal history Gregory VII., Celestine V., John XXII., and others....The league of French seigneurs in 1246 against the clergy, justified themselves on the ground that they were the sons of serfs. Michelet, *Hist. de France*, II. 615. "Not Christians, but Freethinkers, have been the best friends of *despotism*." Lecky, *Hist. of Rat.* II. 245. Renan has remarked on the democratic sympathies of many of the saints. Even the elective principle of representative government—which surely is the strongest bulwark of liberty—is due to the Church. "The 320 Bishops who met at Nice did lawfully represent the multitude of believers, they were the issue of a democratic inspiration." Mazzini, *Letter to Œcumen. Coun., Fortn. Rev.*, 1870. "L'organisation catholique a d'une part attribué graduellement au principe électif une plenitude d'extension jusqu'alors entièrement inconnue...; d'une part, sous un aspect moins apprécié, mais non moins capital, elle a radicalement perfectionné la nature de ce principe politique, en le

(3) And lastly, as to Christianity being superseded by Civilization, the words are meaningless, or if not meaningless, are false. For Civilization means either appliances of comfort, increase of knowledge, refinements of Art, discoveries of Science, diffusion of wealth, and all that may be summed up in the one word—material improvement;—and to these, except that she scorns comfort, frowns on luxury, and discourages the greed for gold—which things are the *dangers* of civilization and not its *blessings*—the Church, as we have seen, is the loftiest aid :—or else Civilization means purer happiness, greater nobleness, clearer and surer wisdom[1]; and if

rendant plus rationnel, par cela seul qu'elle substituait essentiellement désormais le choix réel des inférieurs par les supérieurs," modified however by "les légitimes réclamations des subordonnés." Comte, *Phil. Pos.* v. 346.

[1] See Mill, *Dissert.* II. 161. It is impossible to find in the ideals of any philosophy, even the latest, a single point which is not anticipated and ennobled in Christianity. Does Secularism aim that "all material discoveries should result in the increase of moral force?" (Michelet, *Hist. de France*, II. 622.) Christianity does more, for it furnishes the only means. Or, take any of the Comtist formulæ : is "love their principle, order their basis, progress their end?" so also it is ours: do they impress the noble conceptions of the solidarity, continuity, and totality of life? we add to them Infinity (Comte, *Phil. Pos.* v. *passim* ; Westcott, "Aspects of Positivism," in *Cont. Rev.* VIII. 381). The "liberty that comes spontaneously through nobleness of life" (Bridges, *Unity of Comte's Life and Doctrine*, p. 54), the "sacrifice of self for the good of others" (Congreve, *The Propagation of the New Religion*, p. 21),—"the public and personal care of bodily health, intellectual force, and moral obedience" (*Id.* p. 19),—the "reconcilement of the law of duty to the law of happiness" (Comte, *Catechism of the Pos. Rel.* p. 310),—is there anything here which is lacking to Christianity?

indeed it means these things, then to us it seems that Civilization is but a secular phrase for Christianity itself. Look, my brethren, at your own hearts, their needs and yearnings, their sins and sorrows, their low impulses and heavenly aspirations, and ask whether material progress can do anything to satisfy them, to assuage, to repress, to stimulate ; ask whether material improvement would be anything better than a glistering misery, unless it were guided, interpreted, ennobled by the faith of Christ?

Surely then, to conclude, these were services which, even had their power been exhausted, would deserve our deepest gratitude, and we may exclaim in a very different sense from that of the French Philosopher, "Religion of Christ, behold thy consequences [1]!" But, so far from being exhausted, the realization of these principles is as yet but partial, their power as yet but inchoate.

"We live," says Prof. Huxley, "in a world which is full of misery and ignorance, and the plain duty of each and all of us is to try and make the little corner he can influence somewhat less miserable, and somewhat less ignorant, than it was before he entered it."—The sentence might come from a sermon of Archbishop Manning, or Canon Liddon, or Mr Newman Hall.—" To do this effectually," he adds, " it is necessary to be fully possessed of only two beliefs,— the first, that the order of nature is ascertainable by our faculties to an extent which is practically unlimited ; the second, that our volition counts for something as a condition of the course of events." If we should demur to this exposition, it would not be on religious grounds ; we should desire to modify and supplement, not to supersede it.

[1] " *Religion Chrétienne, violà tes effets!* " Voltaire, after an ingenious calculation that Christianity has cost the lives of some 10,000,000 of men !

For, by the promise of Inspiration, *all* is ours: all the Universe, whether height or depth; all Science, whether she labour in the starry spaces or the microscopical abyss; all History, whether things present or things to come; all Humanity, whether Greek or barbarian, whether bond or free; all the wealth of past Wisdom, all the treasuries of future Hope: ours to study now, ours to possess hereafter; they have been prepared for us through the infinite past, entrusted to us for the brief present, promised to us, in their perfect restitution, for the illimitable future. Whatever Christianity may be, it is at least no narrow dogma, no evanescent influence. As we have seen, it dilates our whole being—corporal, mental, spiritual; it consecrates our whole influence—domestic, social, political; to our partial successes, if they be honourable, it promises future completion; to our total failures, if they be undeserved, it is the pledge of undreamt success. It unites us to Nature, by whose conditions we are bounded, but whose forces we direct. It unites us to the Dead—all saints whom we reverence, all souls whom we commemorate; it unites us to the Living, all whom we love and know not, all whom we love and know; it unites us to Posterity, for which, sustained by Faith, inspired by Hope, we labour with patient unselfishness and active love; above all, and more than all, it unites us to the Infinite by making us the children of God and joint-heirs with Christ, if so be that we suffer with Him. Is this a limited horizon? is this an inadequate consolation? is this an unsatisfying hope? is there nothing here which assures us that we are greater than we know? Is there anything, any religion or irreligion, any philosophy or any ignorance, which can in a greater degree than this

"Give grandeur to the beatings of the heart"?

And is this then a religion to be rejected as obsolete, or despised as immature? No! my brethren, but let us confess with shame, that if any have thought so, the fault has been largely ours. We, alas! have been ignorant and intolerant, we have been narrow and violent, we have been divided and cold. Too little have we understood Christ's doctrine, too little practised His law. Christendom has too often been Christian in name alone. And thus have our idols, as all idols are, been to our own decay. The idol of Power, set up by the ambition of ecclesiastics; the idol of System, to which were reared the vast temples of Scholasticism; the idol of Intellectual Tyranny, to which the altars of the Inquisition smoked with blood; the idol of Self-will, worshipped in common by so many divided sects—these idols have so usurped the Holy Places that they have made the Lord's House to be abhorred. A jealous orthodoxy, a dull letter-worship, a sectarian narrowness, an empty iteration of formulæ, an irritating obtrusion of ceremonies—these things have been the foes of faith. The Pharisees have been worse enemies to it than the Sadducees; the Inquisition than the Infidel. But now, thank God, our Church is more awake to these dangers, and she seeks to remedy the failings alike of her supporters and her foes. Paganism too much obliterated the Individual; Catholicism overlooked too much the element of the World; Science and Philosophy had obscured the conception of God: but it is the duty of our Church, and it is her aim, to reconcile the Individual, the World, and God[1]; to unite, to further, to consecrate the work of her every child. She hails the emancipation of the Intellect; she longs for the Progress of Society; she would hallow both to the glory of God. Oh, as, at this blessed season, we listen in fancy to the Angel-songs, as we lean in fancy with the simple shepherds by the manger-cradle—as there, with the Eastern Magi, we are humbly emulous to lay our choicest gifts—may we pray more and more earnestly from our inmost hearts, that the Kingdom of that beloved Saviour whose birth we commemorate, may indeed come in all its fulness, in all its universality; and may it be given us, like "a deep peace in the heart of a mighty agitation," to realize that, if we be true to ourselves and true to God, nothing can separate us from the love of Christ; that all things are ours, whether the world, or life, or death, or things present, or things to come—all are ours, and we are Christ's, and Christ is God's.

[1] "God, nature, and man—three Cantos in the gigantic religious epopeia, which has the ideal for its subject and the generation for its poet."—Mazzini.

APPENDICES.

APPENDIX·A. Page 4.

On the Diversity of Christian Evidences.

THE Evidences of Christianity are not only numerous, but dissimilar, and independent. " If man's contrivance, or if the favour of accident, could have given to Christianity any of its apparent testimonies, either its miracles or its prophecies, its morals or its propagation, or, if I may so speak, its Founder, there would be no reason to believe, nor even to imagine, that all these appearances of great credibility could be united together by any such causes. If a successful craft could have contrived its public miracles, or so much as the pretence of them, it required another reach of craft and new resources to provide and adapt its prophecies to the same object. Further, it demanded not only a different art but a totally opposite character, to conceive and propagate its admirable morals. Again, the achievement of its propagation, in defiance of the powers and terrors of the world, implied a new energy of personal genius, and other qualities of action than any occuring in the world before. Lastly, the model of the Life of its Founder, in the very description of it, is a work of so much originality and wisdom as could be the offspring only of consummate powers of invention....But the hypothesis sinks under its incredibility. For each of these suppositions of contrivance being arbitrary, as it certainly is, and unsupported, the climax of them is an extravagance. And if the imbecility of Art is foiled in the hypothesis, the combinations of Accident are too vain to be thought of...."

" The whole compass and system of the Christian Evidence unquestionably has nothing like it, nor approaching to it, in the annals of the world. It is a phenomenon standing alone. I assert this on the concession of those who have exalted it, beside their intention, by the impotent comparison by which they have sought to slander and traduce it. For what has been done? Its miracles have been forced into a sort of parallel with some wild unauthenticated relations in the cloudy romance of a Pagan sophist (in the case of Apollonius Tyaneus); or with the vague and insulated pretences of a better history (in the case of Vespasian); or the mask of a detected and defeated imposture among a Roman Catholic sect. Its prophecies have undergone the violence of a similar comparison with the oracles of Heathenism, long ago put to silence, or the legends of a more recent superstition. Its divine morals have been represented as little better than might be derived from the philosophy of a Grecian or Eastern teacher, Socrates or Confucius. Its wonderful progress and propagation, carried without any of the instruments of human power, and in opposition to them, have been matched with the success of the Mahometan heresy effected by the power of the sword. Thus all ages and countries and creeds have been explored with an industry even greater than the success, to furnish the separate materials of such comparisons as the objectors have been able to produce: while the conspicuous and uncontested fact that Christianity unites within itself the signs and indications which no other system, philosophic or religious, does, nor pretended to do, leaves it in possession of a character which repels the indignity of all comparison by the distant and incommensurate pretensions of the things attempted to be put in resemblance with it."—Davison *On Prophecy*, pp. 31, 32.

"The conspiring probabilities of a subject run together into a perfect conviction."—*Ibid.* p. 28.

APPENDIX B.   Page 138.

Confucius.

THE recent valuable work of Dr. Legge on the Life and Teachings of Confucius, contains a translation of the Analects, and enables us to form some conception of the great K'ung Foo-tsze.

A few extracts will show how modest were his own claims compared with those which his followers and worshippers have set up for him.

" The sage and the man of perfect virtue—how dare I rank myself with them? It may be simply said of me *that I strive to become such* without satiety, and teach others without weariness."—*Analects*, VII. 33.

" In letters I am perhaps equal to other men; but the character of the perfect man, carrying out in his conduct what he professes, *is what I have not yet attained to.*"—*Ibid.* 32.

He deliberately placed himself below many of the old sages of China.

" A transmitter," he said, " and not a maker, believing in and loving the ancients, I venture to compare myself with our old P'ang."

He avoided the subjects of God and Immortality, and this is why his influence has been unfavourable to the growth of religion in China.

" He sacrificed to the dead *as if* they were present; he sacrificed to the spirits *as if* the spirits were present."—*Ibid.* III. 12.

His general method was to evade the entire subject, *e.g.*, " Ke Loo asked about serving the spirits of the dead, and the master said, 'While you are not able to serve men, how can you serve their spirits?' The disciple added, 'I venture to ask about death;' he was answered, 'While you do not know about life, how can you know about death?'"—*Ibid.* XI. 11.

"Tsze-Kung asked him, 'Do the dead have knowledge?' The master said, 'You need not wish to know, Tsze, whether the dead have knowledge or not. There is no present urgency about the point. Hereafter you will know it for yourself.'" "I incline to think," adds Dr. Legge, "that he doubted more than he believed." And if so, to what a dreary sham his whole religious prescriptions are reduced!

Two or three further passages will show the opinions of Dr. Legge—and we could have no more competent authority —on his character and teaching.

"There is a want of freedom about the philosopher. Somehow he is less a sage to me after I have seen him at his table, in his undress, in his bed, in his carriage." —*Ibid.* 90.

"As by his frequent references to 'Heaven,' instead of following the phraseology of the older sages, he gave occasion to many of his followers to identify God with a principle of reason and the course of nature, so...he has led them to deny, like the Sadducees of old, the existence of any spirit at all, and to tell us that *their sacrifices to the dead are but an outward form, the mode of expression which the principle of filial piety requires them to adopt when its objects have departed this life.*" —*Ibid.* 102.

"I must now leave the sage. I hope I have not done him injustice. After long study of his character and opinions, I am unable to regard him as a great man. He was not before his age, though he was above the great mass of the officers and scholars of his time. *He threw no new light on any of the questions that have a world-wide interest. He gave no impulse to religion. He had no sympathy with progress.*"—*Ibid.* 115.

APPENDIX C. Page 138.

Buddha.

THE life of Sakya Mouni was singularly noble : "Je n'hésite pas à ajouter," says M. Barthélemy St. Hilaire (*Le Buddha et sa Religion*, Paris, 1860), " que, sauf le Christ tout seul, il n'est point, parmi les fondateurs de religion, de figure plus pure, ni plus touchante que celle du Bouddha. Sa vie n'a point de tâche. Son constant héroïsme égale sa conviction : et si la théorie qu'il préconise est fausse, les exemples personnels qu'il donne sont irréprochables." p. v.

Speaking of the noble missionary Hiouen-thsang—the St. Francis Xavier of Buddhism—Prof. Max Müller says that for four nights and five days he travelled through the desert without a drop of water. " He had nothing to refresh himself except his prayers, and what were they? Texts from a work which taught that there was no God, no Creator, no creation—nothing but mind, minding itself. It is incredible in how exhausted an atmosphere the divine spark within us will glimmer on, and even warm the dark chambers of the human heart."—Max Müller, *Chips*, p. 269.

Buddhism, as a religion, is Atheism fast merging into Idolatry.

" Il n'y a pas trace de l'idée de Dieu dans le Boudhisme entier, ni au début ni au terme."—B. St. Hiliare, p. iv.

" The attribution to a Buddha of power and sanctity infinitely superior to that of the gods is only a development of the notion that the gods could be made subject to the will of a mortal by his performance of superhuman austerities...The notion of Buddha's supremacy once established,

the worship of the gods became superfluous; but as the mass of mankind are in need of sensible objects to which their devotions are to be addressed, Buddha came to be substituted for the gods, and his statues to usurp their altars."
—Wilson, *Essays on the Religion of the Hindoos.*

" In this respect Buddhism was a degeneration from the previous Brahminism, of which in other respects it was a reform."—B. St. Hilaire, p. 164.

It is " a spiritualism without soul, a virtue without duty, a moral without liberty, a charity without love, a world without nature and without God."—*Ibid.* p. 182.

" Insufficient for time and rejecting eternity, the utmost triumph of his religion is to live without fear and to die without hope."—Sir J. Em. Tennant's *Christianity in Ceylon*, p. 227.

The general social effects of Buddhism seem to be purely disastrous.

" There are some peculiar features in the teaching of Sakya and his disciples which render it more surprising that it could ever have been successful, than that its success should have been of temporary duration. *Its object is not the good of the people in their social condition.* It no doubt enjoins the observance of moral duties...but to whom are these injunctions addressed...to Bhikshas...persons who have separated themselves from the world, and who, besides professing faith in Buddha, engage to lead a life of self-denial, celibacy, and mendicancy, and to estrange themselves from all domestic and social obligations."..." In this spirit is the whole of the Vinaya or Buddhist discipline conceived: it is a set of rules for individuals separated from society, in whom all natural feeling is to be suppressed, all passions and desires extinguished, consistently enough with *the doctrine that life is the source of all evil,* and that one means of counteracting it is by checking the increase of living things."
—Wilson, *Essays*, I. 360.

APPENDIX D. Page 144.

Comte.

THE subject of the relations of Comtism to Christianity have been handled in so masterly and admirable a manner by Professor Westcott in the *Contemporary Review* (VI. 399, VIII. 371), that it might be sufficient to refer to those two papers in confirmation of what I have said. I will, however, add a few quotations :—

One of the mottoes of Positivism is *Réorganiser sans Dieu ni roi.*

"Vous prétendez," says Dr. Séméric, "que tout va mal parceque Dieu n'est pas assez parmi nous, tandis que nous affirmons que tout irait bien mieux s'il n'y était pas du tout."—*Positivistes et Catholiques,* p. 13.

"Humanity," says Comte, is "an immense eternal Being, destined by sociological laws to constant development under the preponderating influence of biological and cosmological necessities. *This the real Great Being, on whom all, whether individuals or societies, depend, as the prime mover of their existence,* becomes the centre of our affections."—*Catechism of Positive Religion* (translated by Dr Congreve), p. 64.

His definition of Prayer, which he calls "a work of art," is as follows :—"We adore her (Humanity) *not as his worshipper adored God, with vain compliments,* but *in order to serve her better by bettering ourselves.*"—*Ib.* 106.

"The future of the world," says Dr Congreve, "will justify the faith...that man can be a providence to himself, in a more practical and beneficial sense than any of the various providences he created in his earlier existence; that *Humanity will be found the real, God but the imaginary, source of blessings hitherto attained*, or in the future attainable; and, as such source, the legitimate object of our worship in the Positive sense of that term when freed from theological associations."—*The Propagation of the New Religion* (ad fin.).

One of the passages alluded to in the text may be found in another sermon of Dr Congreve's: *The New Religion in its Attitude to the Old*.

"We take in connection the sum of the conditions of existence, and *we give them an ideal being* and a definite home in *space*, the second great creation, which completes the central one of Humanity. In the bosom of space we place the *World;* and we *conceive of* the World and this our mother Earth as gladly welcomed to that bosom with the simplest and purest love, and we give our love in return... *Thus we complete the Trinity of our Religion—Humanity, the World, Space.*"—P. 18.

Δῖνος βασιλεύει τὸν Δι᾿ ἐξελμλακώς ! Ar. *Nub.* 828.

In the same sermon Dr Congreve says: "We accept; so have all men. We obey; so have all men. We venerate; so have some in past ages and in other countries. *We add but one other term—we love.*"

It is strange that this should be regarded as a new addition to the religious sense of the world; and it is in singular contrast to Comte's own remark :

"I am free to confess, my daughter, that hitherto the Positive Spirit has been tainted with the two moral evils which peculiarly wait on knowledge. *It puffs up and it dries the heart, by giving* free scope to pride and *by turning it from love.*"—*Catechism of Positive Religion*, p. 72.

The religious depth and earnestness of Comte's own spirit was the direct result of Christian teaching, and was probably due in no small degree to his favourite book, the object of his daily study, the *Imitatio Christi*. He says: " I sum up all my wishes for personal perfection in the admirable form by which the sublimest of mystics was led to prepare in his own manner the moral motto of Positivism : *Amem te plus quam me, nec me nisi propter te.*"

THE END.

WORKS BY THE SAME AUTHOR.

THE HISTORY OF INTERPRETATION. Being the Bampton Lectures, 1885. Demy 8vo. 16s.

SERMONS AND ADDRESSES DELIVERED IN AMERICA. With an Introduction by PHILLIPS BROOKS, D.D. Crown 8vo. 7s. 6d.

MERCY AND JUDGMENT. A Few Last Words on Christian Eschatology with reference to Dr. Pusey's "What is of Faith?" Second Edition. Crown 8vo. 10s. 6d.

EPHPHATHA : or, The Amelioration of the World. Sermons preached at Westminster Abbey, with Two Sermons preached in St. Margaret's Church at the Opening of Parliament. Crown 8vo. 6s.

ETERNAL HOPE. Sermons in Westminster Abbey. November and December, 1877. Crown 8vo. 6s.

[*Twenty-fourth Thousand.*

SAINTLY WORKERS. Lent Lectures delivered at St. Andrew's, Holborn. March and April, 1878. New Edition. Crown 8vo. 6s.

SEEKERS AFTER GOD. The lives of SENECA, EPICTETUS, and MARCUS AURELIUS. With Illustrations. New Edition. Crown 8vo. 6s.

"We can heartily recommend it as healthy in tone, instructive, interesting, mentally and spiritually stimulating and nutritious. Mr. Farrar writes as a scholar, a thinker, an earnest Christian, a wise teacher, and a genuine artist."—*Nonconformist.*

"IN THE DAYS OF THY YOUTH." Sermons on Practical Subjects, Preached at Marlborough College, from 1871 to 1876. Seventh Edition. Crown 8vo. 9s.

"These sermons show us the high gifts—intellectual, moral, and spiritual—of their author; we cannot doubt they did help most powerfully to do the work which he had so closely at heart."—*Guardian.*

THE FALL OF MAN : and other Sermons. Fifth Edition. Crown 8vo. 6s.

"Ability, eloquence, scholarship, and practical usefulness are in these sermons combined in a very unusual degree."—*British Quarterly Review.*

THE WITNESS OF HISTORY TO CHRIST. Hulsean Lectures for 1870. Seventh Edition. Crown 8vo. 5s.

"High and earnest in tone, they show reading and thought, and they are full of passages of great eloquence and beauty."—*Guardian.*

THE SILENCE AND VOICES OF GOD. University and other Sermons. Sixth Edition. Crown 8vo. 6s.

"The Sermons are marked by great ability, by an honesty which does not hesitate to acknowledge difficulties, by an earnestness which commands respect."—*Pall Mall Gazette.*

MACMILLAN & CO., LONDON.

BY THE SAME AUTHOR.

GREEK GRAMMAR RULES, drawn up for the use of Harrow School. Eighteenth Edition. 8vo. 1s. 6d.

∗ Now in use in Harrow School, Marlborough College, Rossall School, Uppingham School, Charterhouse School, &c.

A BRIEF GREEK SYNTAX AND HINTS ON GREEK ACCIDENCE ; with some reference to Comparative Philology, and with Illustrations from various Modern Languages. Tenth Edition. 12mo. 4s. 6d.

"Mr. Farrar's volume surpasses all the Greek Grammars we have seen."—*Educational Times.*

"This book is the produce of the ripest scholarship. Though his main object is to treat of Syntax, the space he devotes to comparative philology, and the copious illustrations he gives from various modern languages, increase greatly the value of the book. At the same time his practical experience in teaching his class at Harrow has given him a familiarity with the difficulties that beset beginners, and enables him most successfully to adapt his teaching to their wants. We can most cordially recommend the book."—*Papers for the Schoolmaster.*

LANGUAGE AND LANGUAGES ; being "Chapters on Language" and "Families of Speech." With 2 Philological Maps and 3 Tables of Languages. New Edition. Crown 8vo. 6s.

CHAPTERS ON LANGUAGE.

"Dr. Farrar's volume contains the fruit of much learned thought, and of much study of other learned men's studies. The book is written plainly and intelligibly, and is full of a large human interest."—*Examiner.*

FAMILIES OF SPEECH.

"We fully believe that Dr. Farrar's book is by far the best account as yet given in English, within the same compass, of the history, results, methods, and aspirations of comparative philology or glossology."—*Pall Mall Gazette.*

London : LONGMANS, GREEN, & CO.

THE EARLY DAYS OF CHRISTIANITY. Ninth Thousand. Two Vols. 24s. Popular Edition, 6s.

THE LIFE AND WORK OF ST. PAUL. Nineteenth Thousand. Two Vols. 8vo. 24s. Illustrated Edition, 21s. Popular Edition, 6s.

THE LIFE OF CHRIST. Thirty-first Edition. Library Edition. Two Vols. 8vo. Price 24s. Illustrated Edition, cloth, 21s. ; calf or morocco, £2 2s. Popular Edition, 6s. Bijou Edition, 10s. 6d.

MY OBJECT IN LIFE. (Heart Chords Series.) 1s.

London : CASSELL & COMPANY, LIMITED.

THE GOSPEL OF ST. LUKE. Fcap. 8vo. 4s. 6d.
(Cambridge Bible for Schools.)

London : THE CAMBRIDGE WAREHOUSE.

www.ingramcontent.com/pod-product-compliance
Lightning Source LLC
Chambersburg PA
CBHW031831230426
43669CB00009B/1312